D1104938

INTRODUCTION

TO THE

THEORY OF EMPLOYMENT

INTRODUCTION

TO THE

THEORY OF EMPLOYMENT

BY

Mrs. JOAN ROBINSON

MACMILLAN AND CO., LIMITED
ST. MARTIN'S STREET, LONDON
1938

SYRACUSE UNIVERSITY LIBRARY

COPYRIGHT

First Edition 1937
Reprinted 1938

PRINTED IN GREAT BRITAIN
BY R. & R. CLARK, LIMITED, EDINBURGH

330.1
R61
HB
171
R34
1938

FOREWORD

THE purpose of this book is to provide a simplified account of the main principles of the Theory of Employment for students who find that they require some help in assimilating Mr. Keynes' *General Theory of Employment, Interest and Money*, and the literature which is growing round it. In writing a book of this kind there is necessarily a conflict between the claims of rigour and of simplicity. In the present case it is rigour that has been sacrificed where need be, and the reader must regard this book merely as a preparation for deeper studies. Besides the *General Theory*, I have drawn upon my own *Essays in the Theory of Employment*, Mr. Colin Clark's *National Income and Outlay* and Mr. Michal Kalecki's article, " A Theory of the Business Cycle ", in the *Review of Economic Studies*, February 1937. I have done my best to resist the temptation to address my colleagues over the heads of the audience for which this book is properly intended, and it is not designed to help in the resolution of the controversies which are at present disturbing the world of academic economics.

JOAN ROBINSON

CAMBRIDGE
August 1937

235329

CONTENTS

CHAPTER I

CHAPTER II

CHAPTER III

CHAPTER IV

CHAPTER V

CHAPTER VI

CHAPTER VII

CHAPTER VIII

CHAPTER IX

CONTENTS

CHAPTER I

INTRODUCTION

INTRODUCTORY

THE modern economic system fails to provide employment continuously for all who desire to work. This is generally recognised as one of the major defects of the system, and remedies for the defect are constantly being propounded. Diagnosis must precede prescription, and the following pages attempt to do no more than to assist the reader to the first elementary stages of an understanding of the disease.

The reader may be inclined to ask, " If it is possible to understand what causes trade prosperity, why do we not immediately set about to secure it ? " That, indeed, is a hard question. Economic life presents us always with a choice of evils and no course of policy is the best for everyone. There will always be some who prefer the disease to any possible treatment that can be proposed for it, and the question of remedies remains in dispute even when the diagnosis is agreed upon. This volume is intended to guide the reader towards an understanding of the problem, but not to tell him what ought to be done.

1

DEFICIENCY OF DEMAND

Under a system of private enterprise it is, in a simple and obvious sense, the decisions of employers—in the main, industrial entrepreneurs—which determine the amount of employment offered to the working population, but the entrepreneurs themselves are subject to general influences which cause them to decide one way or another, and the decisions of each influence the decisions of the rest. There is no central control, no plan of action, and whatever actually occurs in economic life is the result of innumerable independent individual decisions. The course which it is best for each individual to pursue in his own interests is rarely the same as the course best calculated to promote the interests of society as a whole, and if our economic system appears sometimes fantastic or even insane—as when foodstuffs are destroyed while men go hungry—we must remember that it is not surprising that the interaction of free individual decisions should lead so often to irrational, clumsy and bewildering results.

Under this system, goods and services are produced in order that they may be sold profitably. Thus the output of goods and services that will be produced depends upon the demand for them. " Demand " implies money expenditure, not desire or need. No matter how great a man's need may be for goods to feed and clothe and amuse him, he cannot make it worth anyone's

2

while to produce them for him unless he has money to pay, and need does not constitute " demand " unless it is accompanied by expenditure. As we know only too well, in the economic system under which we live, it often happens that productive resources are unemployed—men out of work, machines idle, land falling out of cultivation—while at the same time there is bitter need for the goods which they are able to produce. Output falls below its possible maximum, not when needs are satiated, but when demand is deficient.

How can a deficiency of demand come about? The demand for goods on the part of individual consumers is governed mainly by their income. The larger the income an individual has the greater will be his expenditure on current consumption. But income is the product of expenditure as well as the source of expenditure. Men earn their incomes by supplying each other's demands. One man's expenditure provides other men's incomes, and one man's income is derived from other men's expenditure. From this we might be inclined to argue that if resources are idle at any moment it must be the result merely of accident or mismanagement, for all that is necessary is to increase activity, and incomes will increase so as to provide a demand for the extra goods produced.

But the whole of everyone's income is not spent on current consumption. Provided the standard of life of an individual is above a certain bare minimum, he may want to save part of his

3

income in order to build up a store of wealth.
Wealth is accumulated in order to provide
security against future emergencies, to satisfy
the lust of possession, or to acquire further
income by lending it at interest. For motives of
this kind, individuals put aside part of their
income, and acquire wealth, by means of consuming less than the full amount of goods which
their income could purchase. This would cause
no trouble if the decision to save led directly to
a demand for real capital—houses, machines,
ships and so forth. For in that case the part of
income saved would give employment in making
capital goods just as the part spent on consumption gives employment in making consumption goods. The desire to save could not
then be a cause of unemployment.

But the demand for capital goods comes, not
from saving, but from business concerns who use
them in production, and no entrepreneur is
inclined to acquire capital goods unless he can
see a profit by doing so. The mere fact that
individuals want to save part of their incomes to
add to their private wealth does nothing to
encourage entrepreneurs to expect a greater
profit from capital. The profitability of capital
goods depends upon the demand for the consumption goods which they produce. Thus if individuals decide to save, that is, not to spend on
immediate consumption, they reduce rather than
increase the motive of the entrepreneurs for
acquiring new capital goods, and the decision to

save reduces the demand for consumption goods without increasing the demand for capital goods.

It is for this reason that unemployment can occur. There is unemployment when the decisions of entrepreneurs as to how much new capital it is worth their while to acquire fall short of the desire of individuals to save. Saving depletes the demand for consumption goods, for saving means not spending upon current consumption, and the entrepreneurs fail to make up for it by creating a sufficient demand for capital goods to fill the gap. Then demand is deficient and men and machines stand idle, not because humanity has no *need* for their services, but because *demand* is not great enough for anyone to be able to make a profit for himself by setting them to work.

Synopsis

The next four chapters will be devoted to following out the clue which we have here picked up—that the level of demand, and consequently of employment, depends upon the interaction between the desire to save and the desire to invest in real capital. Chapter II (Investment and Saving) outlines this system of ideas. Chapter III (The Multiplier) describes in more detail the effect of a change in investment upon employment and Chapter IV discusses the reasons for which a change in investment may occur. Chapter V (Changes in Thriftiness) is devoted to the desire to save. We are now possessed of the major part of the theory of employment, but there are some more pieces of the jig-saw puzzle which must be collected before we can make a complete picture. Prices and the monetary system have still to be considered. After glancing at some miscellaneous points in Chapter VI, we turn to the subject of the price level in Chapter VII. Chapter VIII introduces the important topic of the rate of interest, and shows in what way the workings of the monetary system are connected with the influences which determine employment. The next two chapters (Aspects of the Rate of Interest and Changes in the Supply of Money) are each, in a certain sense, a digression from our main theme, though the matters with which they deal are of great importance. Chapter XI (Foreign Trade), treating briefly a subject which requires a volume to itself, shows how the matters which we have been discussing from the point of view of the world appear differently when we look at them from the point of view of a single country. Chapter XII (Changes in Employment) gathers the various pieces together and provides a picture of the oscillations of employment in the modern economic system.

Certain controversial points are discussed in the course of the argument (particularly in the Appendixes, to Chapter X on the Quantity Theory of Money and to Chapter XI on Free Trade), but as far as possible controversy has been avoided. Some reflections on economic controversy are put forward in the last chapter.

CHAPTER II

INVESTMENT AND SAVING

TERMINOLOGY

THE concept of *investment* plays an important part in the argument which follows, and it is necessary at the outset to be clear about terms. By *investment* is meant an addition to real capital, such as occurs when a new house or a new factory is built, a railway line constructed or a store of raw materials accumulated. This use of the word does not correspond to the everyday sense in which investment means merely acquiring a title to capital. In ordinary speech we may say " I have invested £100 in Home Rails ", but in the present context " investment " does not mean buying a piece of paper, but making an addition to the stock of goods in existence. You are not investing when you buy a security; you are investing when you cause a house to be built.

The word *saving*, on the other hand, is used in its ordinary sense. Saving is the difference between income and expenditure upon current consumption. *Income* also is used in its everyday sense. Refined complications have been raised in connection with the definition of these terms, but for our present purposes a rough-and-ready treatment will suffice.

All income is derived ultimately from selling goods and services. It may be derived by working for wages or salaries, or from owning property, land or capital equipment, which contributes to the output of goods, or from lending money, in which case interest is paid out of receipts derived from selling goods and services, or from gifts or allowances from people who derive income from one of these sources. All income, therefore, is derived either from providing for current consumption or from adding to the stock of wealth, that is, from investment. The work of repairing and renewing existing capital goods is best regarded as part of the process of producing consumption goods, and incomes derived from such activities must not be reckoned as investment incomes.

EQUALITY OF INVESTMENT AND SAVING

We have already seen that an individual who adds to his private wealth by saving, that is by consuming less than the whole of his income, does nothing to encourage the production of more real capital, in short that saving in itself does not cause investment to take place. But yet it can easily be seen that for the community as a whole the rate of saving must be equal to the rate of investment. All incomes are derived either from producing consumption goods or from producing investment goods. And all income either is spent

8

on consumption goods or is saved. The income derived from producing consumption goods is equal to what is spent on them. Therefore what is saved is equal to the income derived from producing investment goods. In short, the rate of saving is equal to the rate of investment.

To look at the same thing in another way : each individual who saves adds to his wealth, while any individual who spends more than his income—that is, dis-saves—reduces his wealth, either by getting rid of part of his past accumulation or by increasing his indebtedness. The sum of all the savings, positive and negative, of individuals is the total increase in wealth of the community, and the increase in wealth of the community, over any period, is the investment which has taken place in that period.

But saving is not the same thing as investment. To say that the rate of saving is equal to the rate of investment, for all individuals taken together, does not mean that each individual act of saving leads to a corresponding act of investment. Every individual is free to spend or save his income just as he pleases. His motives for saving are governed by such influences as prudence, family feeling, pride, or inability to think of a new way of spending money. At the same time every entrepreneur is free to decide how much it is worth while to invest in creating new capital goods, having regard to the prospects of profit. Decisions to save and decisions to invest are taken quite independently of each other, and

9

for a quite different class of motives.

In some individual cases the two decisions are bound together, as when a man cuts down his consumption in order to save up and have a house built for himself. But normally even private building is done out of borrowing or out of accumulated wealth, not at the expense of current consumption. Again, in a society different from our own the decision to save and the decision to invest in creating new capital goods may be tied together. Under a completely socialist system the government would decide how much investment was desirable, and would control the amount of collective saving accordingly. Or, in a primitive community, with no money and no borrowing, saving can only take the form of adding to the stock of goods owned by the individual family. When the family desire to save more, they eat up less of the year's crop and retain a larger stock in their barns.

But in the system under which we live the decision to save and the decision to invest are not bound together, and the motives governing them are quite different. How then does it come about that, on balance, individuals always decide to save just as much as entrepreneurs have decided to invest?

What Happens when Investment Increases

Let us suppose that in a time of general unemployment entrepreneurs decide to extend their plant at a greater rate than formerly, while the desire of individuals to save remains the same. An increase in activity now takes place in the capital-good industries. Incomes increase—men formerly unemployed begin to receive wages and profits go up. Part of these additional incomes are spent, activity in the consumption-good industries also increases, and a further increase in incomes takes place.

Now, with a higher level of income, and the same general attitude to saving as before, the amount that people save will increase. For without any change in the general state of family affection, foresight and pride—without, that is to say, any change in the desire to save—people will save more when their incomes are higher. A change in the desire to save means that people are inclined to save more out of the same income. But with the same desire to save, the actual amount of saving will depend upon the income they have to dispose of. As the most urgent needs are met, and the standard of life becomes more comfortable, the importance of present consumption grows less compared to the advantages of owning wealth, and the moral effort of refraining from present consumption becomes less strenuous. Thus, as a general rule, saving increases with income. This rule does not apply to every individual, nor to any one individual in all circumstances, but, as we should expect, it is found to hold good by and large.

Saving depends upon income, and income

11

depends upon the rate at which investment goods are being produced. Everyone is free to save as much as he likes, but how much he likes to save is influenced by his income, and his income is influenced by the decisions of entrepreneurs as to how much it is worth their while to invest. Thus everyone does what he likes, but what he likes is determined for him by the entrepreneurs. Saving is equal to investment, because investment leads to a state of affairs in which people want to save. Investment causes incomes to be whatever is required to induce people to save at a rate equal to the rate of investment. The more willing people are to save, the lower is the level of income corresponding to a given rate of investment, and the smaller the increase in income brought about by a given increase in the rate of investment.

What Happens when the Desire to Save Increases

The argument does not run in the reverse way. The desire to save does not promote investment. Let us suppose that individuals' desire to save increases—that is, the amount they will save out of a given income goes up—while entrepreneurs are undertaking investment at the same rate as before. Then, some individuals will spend less of their income than formerly. Activity and income in the consumption-good trades will therefore fall off. Owing to this decline in income, consumption will be further curtailed, and a further decline in incomes will take place. One man's expenditure is other men's income, and when one man spends less, other men earn less. As incomes fall the amount that individuals want to save is cut down, and income for the community as a whole is reduced to the level at which the actual rate of saving is no greater than the rate of investment. The more reluctant people are to cut down their saving, the greater will be the fall in incomes.

Thus we see once more that whatever the attitude of individuals to saving may be, the amount that they will actually save, taken together, is determined for them by the decisions of the entrepreneurs as to the amount of investment goods that it suits them to produce. Any one individual, it is true, can increase his rate of saving, but the very fact that he is saving more, which means that he is spending less, leads to a decline in other people's incomes to such an extent that they save less, and his saving makes no change in the total rate of saving. The individual saver has no direct influence upon the rate of investment. If entrepreneurs see a profit to be made by investment, investment will take place, and if they do not it will not. The initiative lies with the entrepreneurs, not with the savers. The savers, as a group, are helpless in the hands of the entrepreneurs, though any one individually is free to save as much as he likes. If the desire of individuals to save increases, but the desire of entrepreneurs to create new capital goods does not increase, then no increase in the rate of aggregate saving can take place and the impulse to save runs to waste. Consumption falls off, and incomes decline as much as consumption, so that in spite of the sacrifices of increased thrift no increase in saving takes place; abstinence brings no reward of added wealth to the community. The actions and decisions of the savers can have no direct effect upon the rate at which new capital goods are created. All that they can influence directly is the level of current consumption and current output of consumption goods, and so the level of income and total activity.

THE " HOARDING " FALLACY

Some writers appear to disagree with this view. Savings, they say, are devoted to buying securities, and if saving increases there is an increased demand for securities. New securities are issued in order to finance investment, and therefore an increase in saving leads to an increase in investment. This argument sinks at the first step, for, since an individual, by increasing his own savings, reduces the savings of others, he does not add to the rate of saving of the community, and therefore does not add to the demand for securities. But the initial error leads to a further complication. If saving directly caused investment, it would be very difficult to see how unemployment could possibly occur, and such writers, in order to provide an explanation of unemployment, usually fall back on the notion of " hoarding ". If an individual saves, they say, and buys securities with his new wealth, investment automatically increases, but if he puts his new wealth into money, that is, hoards it, there is no corresponding investment. But this is simply an error. The saving of the individual is not a cause of investment in either case, and the distinction does not arise. We shall find, it is true, that the desire of individuals to hold their wealth (whether newly saved or owned for some time makes no difference) in money rather than securities plays an important part in influencing the rate of investment, *via* the rate of interest. But this is an indirect and complicated effect. The individual saver has no direct influence on the rate of investment, whether he buys securities or not. He may buy securities or add to his holding of money, whichever he pleases, but since other people are saving less because he is saving more they are buying less securities or parting with money they formerly held. The question of how wealth is held, whether in money or securities, has only the slightest connection with the interaction of investment and saving.

The error connected with the idea of " hoarding " arises, no doubt, from the desire to find where the vanished savings have got to. It is clear enough that if the desire of individuals to save has increased, but the desire of entrepreneurs to invest has not increased, then actually savings do not increase, and the explanation is put forward that the missing savings have somehow got lost on the way by going into money instead of into securities. But this is not a tenable explanation. The savings are nowhere. They have failed to come into existence, because as fast as one man increases his saving, by reducing his spending, other men's incomes fall off and they save less as much as he saves more. It is of no use to search for the non-existent savings either in " hoards " or anywhere else.

SUMMARY

To sum up : When investment increases, incomes rise to the point at which saving increases equally, but if the desire to save increases, incomes fall off so much that on balance saving is no greater than before. It is through changes in income that the equality of saving and investment is preserved. Thus the level of income is determined by the rate of investment and the desire to save ; given the desire to save, the level of income that will rule is governed by the rate of investment. And given the rate of investment the level of income is determined by the desire to save.

We are now able to give a provisional account of how it comes about that resources can be wasted in idleness. If the amount that entrepreneurs in given conditions are willing to invest is less than the amount that individuals, taken

16

together, would want to save out of the incomes which the full employment of resources would entail, then there cannot be full employment, and incomes will in fact be less than they would be if full employment obtained. Or to look at the same thing in another way—suppose that the investment decisions of entrepreneurs have been taken, in the light of expected future profit. Then the current rate of investment is given, and if individuals are not willing to spend on current consumption the whole difference between the rate of investment and the total of income that there would be if there were full employment, then there will not be full employment.

Thus the popular description of unemployment as " poverty in the midst of plenty " contains a large element of truth, for in one sense unemployment arises because the incomes which some individuals would enjoy, in the absence of unemployment, would be so large that they would not want to spend enough money to make it profitable for entrepreneurs to give everyone employment who wants to work.

This is merely a provisional account of matters which will become clearer as our argument proceeds.

CHAPTER III

THE MULTIPLIER

PRIMARY AND SECONDARY EMPLOYMENT

WE must now consider in more detail the effect of an increase in investment upon income and upon saving. When an increase in investment takes place, say in house-building, at a time of general unemployment, men are given jobs in building, in making materials, such as bricks, glass and door-knobs, and in transport. The additional employment thus given is the *primary* increase in employment due to the increase in investment. When employment increases the men concerned increase their rate of consumption—buying more boots and shirts and bacon and cheese. Similarly, when more profits are being made by building contractors and so forth, the individuals whose incomes have increased will spend more upon consumption goods. Thus employment will increase, and more profits will be earned, in making the boots and other goods for which the market has now improved. The boot operatives, in turn, have more money to spend when they are taken into work, shareholders receive larger dividends, the shops and cinemas and garages make bigger profits. With larger incomes being earned in the consumption-good industries a further increase in consumption takes place, and employment and profits, in making boots and selling petrol and the rest, increase still further. Larger incomes again lead to more consumption, and so on round and round. The addition to employment in the consumption-good industries is the *secondary* increase in employment due to the increase in investment.

At each round the addition to employment and to incomes is less than at the last. The receiver of profits increases his rate of saving when his income increases, so that less than the whole of the additional profits earned at each round is used to increase consumption. And only a part of the wage which a man receives when he finds work is an addition to his income. Even when he was unemployed he was not living on air. He may have been receiving unemployment benefit, relief payments, or assistance from friends or from charity, or he may have kept body and soul together by drawing on his own past accumulated savings, by pawning his furniture or getting into debt to shopkeepers. For convenience we will describe the income of the unemployed, from whatever source it may be drawn, as *dole* income. Part of the expenditure which a man makes when he earns wages merely replaces the dole which he was spending while he was unemployed. Thus less than the whole outlay upon house-building is passed on to the

19

consumption-good industries at the second round and less than the whole of the additional incomes received at the second round is passed on at the third round, and so forth.

The extent to which income is passed on from round to round governs the increase in employment. The ratio of the total increase in employment to the primary increase is known as the *Multiplier*. If, for example, there is an increase in employment of two men in consumption-good industries for every man newly employed in capital-good industries, then the Multiplier is equal to 3.

SAVING EQUATED TO INVESTMENT

The very fact that the whole increase of income is not passed on at each round means that at each round there is an increase in the rate of saving. First, there is an increase of saving out of profits at each stage. Secondly, a reduction in dole payments leads to an increase in saving or decrease in dis-saving. Part or the whole of unemployment relief may be financed by borrowing by the state, and if the state is spending more than it is receiving from taxes, and borrowing the difference, the effect is exactly the same as if an individual is spending more than his income and so reducing his wealth or increasing his indebtedness. When the dole is provided from taxation, so that a reduction in dole payments leads to a remission of taxes, saving by taxpayers increases when a decline in dole payments reduces the burden of taxation. Part of the dole may come from dis-saving or borrowing by the unemployed themselves or by their friends, and charitable individuals may save more when claims upon them are reduced. Thus, one way and another, a reduction in dole payments leads to a reduction in dis-saving or an increase in saving.

It is obvious that, whatever happens, the increase in saving which people, taken together, are induced to make when their incomes are increased as a result of the greater rate of house-building, must be equal to the increased outlay on house-building. For whatever is not saved is spent. If the whole of the outlay on house-building were added to saving at the first round, there would be no second round. In so far as the individuals directly concerned in the house-building increase their consumption, they increase their rate of saving by less than their incomes have increased, that is, by less than the outlay on house-building. But precisely because they do not increase their savings as much as their income has increased, they cause an increase in the incomes, and consequently the savings, of the people concerned in making additional goods for them to consume. And in so far as these people, in turn, save less than the whole addition to their incomes, they cause the incomes of others to increase. Thus the increase in incomes must necessarily continue up to the point at which there is an addition to saving equal to the additional outlay on house-building.

EXAMPLES

To take a simplified example, let us suppose (1) that half of all incomes is wage incomes, and the other half profits ; (2) that out of an addition to profits one-third is saved ; (3) that the whole of wages is spent upon consumption goods ; (4) that the dole of an unemployed man is equal to one-third of the wage of an employed man ; (5) that the whole of dole incomes is provided by borrowing. Then for every additional £1 per week spent upon house-building, wages at the first round are increased by £$\frac{1}{2}$ per week, and profits by £$\frac{1}{2}$. The consumption of wage earners is increased by $\frac{2}{3}$ of the wage, that is by £$\frac{1}{3}$; and consumption by the recipients of profits is increased by £$\frac{1}{3}$. Thus incomes at the second round are increased by £$\frac{2}{3}$, the additional expenditure coming from those whose incomes are increased at the first round. Wages at the second round are increased by £$\frac{1}{3}$, profits by £$\frac{1}{3}$, and expenditure on consumption goods by £$\frac{4}{9}$; and so forth.

Thus, for every £1 per week added to outlay on house-building there is an addition to income, for the community as a whole, of

$$£1+\tfrac{2}{3}+\tfrac{4}{9}+\tfrac{8}{27}+\ldots\ldots,\quad \text{a total of £3 per week,}$$

and for every man newly employed in house-building, 2 men are given employment in the consumption-good industries. In this example the Multiplier is 3, that is to say, the total increase in employment is three times the primary increase in employment in building and providing housing materials.

For every £1 per week spent on house-building there is a reduction, at the first round, of £$\frac{1}{6}$ in dole payments, and an increase of £$\frac{1}{6}$ in saving from profits. We are supposing that the whole of the dole represents dis-saving. Thus there is a net increase in saving, at the first round, of £$\frac{1}{3}$. £$\frac{2}{3}$ of additional income at the second round reduces dole payments by £$\frac{1}{9}$, and causes saving out of profits to increase by £$\frac{1}{9}$, and so on. Thus the total increase in net saving per week is equal to

$$£\tfrac{1}{3}(1) + \tfrac{1}{3}(\tfrac{2}{3}) + \tfrac{1}{3}(\tfrac{4}{9}) + \ldots, \quad \text{a total of £1 per week.}$$

Thus for every £1 added to outlay on house-building £1 is added to saving.

To take another example, suppose that part of wages is saved, let us say one-sixth (that is, a quarter of the difference between the wage and the dole), and that half of the addition to profits is saved. The series for income now becomes

$$£1 + \tfrac{1}{2} + \tfrac{1}{4} + \tfrac{1}{8} + \ldots, \quad \text{and the Multiplier is 2.}$$

Once more saving is increased pound for pound with the increase in investment, for the series for saving now becomes

$$£\tfrac{1}{2}(1) + \tfrac{1}{2}(\tfrac{1}{2}) + \tfrac{1}{2}(\tfrac{1}{4}) + \ldots, \quad \text{a total of £1.}$$

Thus we find, as we have already seen, that however willing or reluctant the community may be to save, the rate of saving is always equal to the rate of investment. Greater willingness to save checks the increase in incomes, and reduces the size of the Multiplier, but it cannot increase the saving that is brought about by an increase in investment.

THE SIZE OF THE MULTIPLIER

We are now able to see the main influences which determine the size of the Multiplier. The Multiplier will be larger the smaller is the addition to saving made from an addition to profits (a third of additional profits in our first example, and half in our second). And since wages are more fully spent than profits, the Multiplier will be larger the greater is the ratio of wages to profits (half in both examples). Only the difference between the wage and the dole is added to the income of a worker when he finds employment, and the lower the ratio of the dole to the wage (a third in both examples) the larger will the Multiplier tend to be.

In our first example we assumed that the whole of wages is spent, in the second that one-sixth is saved. Saving out of wages depends very much upon the immediate past history of the families concerned. An unemployed man may keep body and soul together partly by getting into debt, by drawing on past accumulations, or by pawning his goods. When he finds work he will want to pay off his debts, store up his nest-egg again and redeem his pledges. As time goes by, debts are paid off and expenditure tends to increase. This is one reason, amongst many, why we should not expect the value of the Multiplier to be the same at all times. Its value depends upon the particular situation at the moment when investment increases, and if a steady rate of investment is kept up over a period of time the total of employment will gradually alter.

It is also necessary to consider the manner in which dole payments are provided for. In our examples we assumed that they were entirely financed by borrowing. If the dole which an un-employed man receives comes from the income of other people, whether through taxation or from charity, then those people are likely to increase their own consumption when they are relieved from the necessity of providing for the unemployed. Thus the Multiplier will be larger if the dole is financed by taxation which is remitted when unemployment is reduced than if it is financed entirely by borrowing.

THE MULTIPLIER IN ONE COUNTRY

We have so far discussed the Multiplier from the point of view of the world as a whole. If we are interested only in the increase in employment in the home country when investment at home

INTRODUCTION TO THE THEORY OF EMPLOYMENT

increases, we must make an allowance for imports. When employment at home increases, and expenditure on consumption goods goes up, part of this increase in expenditure will fall on foreign-produced goods, and part of the secondary increase in employment, due to the investment at home, will take place outside the home country. If the newly employed bricklayer buys foreign boots, part of the secondary employment and secondary profits, due to house-building in Cambridge, goes to Czecho-Slovakia instead of to Northampton, and when he buys a shirt, part of the secondary employment and profits go to America, where the raw cotton is grown. Thus the Multiplier for one country alone is smaller than the Multiplier for the world as a whole.

The actual value of the Multiplier, in particular countries in particular circumstances, is a matter of great interest and importance. Two methods can be used to estimate it. One, illustrated in our examples (though these were highly simplified), is to form a reasonable guess at the magnitudes involved, the ratio of wages to profits, of the dole to the wage, of saving to profits, and so forth, and to work out the appropriate geometrical progression. The other method is to study actual changes in employment in capital-good industries and in industry in general and discover the ratio between them. These methods are both being used, and have been found to give reasonably consonant results. It appears that in a period of depression such as 1931 to 1935 in this country the Multiplier was round about 2, while, as we should expect, the Multiplier for U.S.A., which is much less dependent upon imports, was considerably larger.

CHAPTER IV

CHANGES IN INVESTMENT

The Inducement to Invest

WE have seen that the rate of investment plays an essential part in determining the level of employment and incomes at any moment. What determines the rate of investment ? Once more we shall consider the problem from the point of view of the world as a whole. The question of investment in a single country will be treated later.

Entrepreneurs acquire capital goods with a view to using them to produce consumption goods or other capital goods which can be sold at a profit, and the main considerations which govern the demand for them are their expected future earnings and the ruling rate of interest. If the expected earnings of a machine reckoned as a percentage on its cost, allowing for expenses of upkeep and for risk, works out at more than the ruling rate of interest, then there will be a demand for that sort of machine, for it will be profitable to borrow money and order the machine. In the main the same considerations govern the purchase of a machine out of a firm's own resources, for it is folly to sacrifice the interest which would be earned on a sum of money by lending it or holding securities with it, in order to purchase a machine which will earn less. Thus the rate of investment is governed by prospective profits compared to the rate of interest.

To look at the same thing in another way, the price of existing capital goods is determined by their expected earnings and the rate of interest, and it will be profitable to produce new capital goods so long as their cost of production does not exceed this price. Suppose that a certain type of house in a certain town can be let for £60 a year, of which £10 must be spent on upkeep to maintain it permanently in good repair. Then the net earnings of the house is £50 a year. When the rate of interest is 5 per cent. this house is worth £1000, for no one will give more (or accept less) than £1000 for something which yields an income of £50 a year when £50 a year can be obtained as interest on £1000. At 6 per cent. the house is worth £833, at 4 per cent. £1250. Now, if such a house costs £1000 to build, it will be just worth while to build new houses of this type when the rate of interest is 5 per cent. If the rate of interest were 6 per cent. no more such houses would be built, while if the rate of interest were 4 per cent. a building boom would set in. The rate of interest is thus an extremely important influence upon investment. What determines the rate of interest will be discussed in a later chapter.

PROSPECTIVE PROFITS

Estimates of the future earnings of capital goods must, in the nature of the case, be based largely upon guess-work, and investment will increase if, for any reason, expectations of future earnings of capital goods become more cheerful. Thus a revival of confidence as to the future state of trade has an extremely important effect in promoting investment. We here catch a glimpse of one of the causes of the instability of a system of private enterprise. For the current level of demand for consumption goods is an important influence upon the prospective earnings of capital equipment. But an increase in the rate at which capital goods are being produced itself, as we have seen, raises the demand for consumption goods. Thus any upward or downward movement in activity tends to amplify itself up to a certain point.

The prospective earnings of capital goods also depend upon the amount in existence. If an earthquake suddenly destroys part of a city the houses which remain standing become more valuable, and there will be a profit to be made by building new houses. The same principle is at work, in a milder way, in normal times. If slump conditions have been so bad that it has not seemed worth while even to renew old equipment as it wears out, then one fine day entrepreneurs will wake up to the fact that the old equipment which remains has become more

valuable, and new equipment will begin to be
ordered. Conversely, as capital accumulates
more and more equipment is competing to
satisfy a given demand for consumption goods,
and the rate of profit on capital falls off.

Thus there is a rhythmical tendency in investment. When slump conditions have continued for a certain time investment begins to
revive. The mere fact that investment has begun
to increase raises the level of activity and so
fires the hope of future profit from investment.
The upward movement continues to feed upon
itself until the accumulation of capital de-
presses the rate of profit. Hope turns to pessimism and a downward movement begins, which
will once more reverse itself after a certain time
has elapsed.

So long as population is increasing, new inventions are constantly being made, and new
territories opened up to trade, the demand for
capital goods is constantly expanding, independently of the rhythmical rise and fall of activity.
In such conditions slumps will be less severe and
will come to an end more quickly than when
population and technical knowledge are stable.
It is mainly for this reason that unemployment
was a less serious problem in the nineteenth
century than it is to-day. For in the nineteenth
century the western economic world was expanding in every way, so that the demand for
new capital was always running ahead faster
than investment could catch up upon it, and

prospective profits never fell very low, or remained low for very long.

Public Investment

A large amount of investment, in such things as improvements in roads, school buildings, extensions of telephone equipment, playing-fields, gas-works and so forth, is undertaken by the state and local authorities. These are not subject to the profit motive in the same direct way as private investment, and do not necessarily follow the same rhythm. Some of them, such as a municipal gas-works, yield a money return, but others, such as recreation grounds, are undertaken with a view to a benefit to the community which does not show itself directly in money receipts. Another kind of state investment is the provision of armaments.

All these kinds of investment produce an immediate effect, while incomes are being earned in constructing the capital works, upon the current demand for consumption goods, which is of exactly the same nature as that produced by investment undertaken by profit-seeking entrepreneurs. The immediate effect upon employment of a scheme of investment is nothing whatever to do with the usefulness or earning-power of the capital goods produced. When the Tower of Babel was being built a large number of men were engaged upon an entirely unproductive enterprise, but while they were at

work they had to be clothed and fed; their
wages were spent upon the current output of
consumption-good industries, which must have
enjoyed a boom while the building was going on,
and suffered a violent slump when the project
was abandoned.

It is of course always desirable on general
grounds that employment in the capital-good
industries should be turned to the best advantage
and be used for making valuable capital goods,
which will add to future wealth, instead of being
used for foolish projects, but the immediate
effect upon employment is in no way enhanced
by the future usefulness of the capital works.
This is a fact which the public in general find it
somewhat hard to grasp. There is a strong moral
resistance against believing that a piece of investment that is useless, or even harmful, in its long-
run aspect, can be beneficial in the sense of
increasing employment and income while it is
going on. But there is no getting away from the
fact that employment will be increased when
investment increases, whether the investment is
useful or not. The application of this argument
to investment in armaments is obvious.

Now, when unemployment is rife, the cost to
a government of a given piece of investment
—say building a road—is very much less than
the actual outlay made upon the road. For
when employment increases, in road-building,
in quarrying to provide materials, and in consumption-good industries catering for the extra

expenditure of individuals engaged in road-building and quarrying, the responsibility of the government and local authorities for unemployment allowances is thereby reduced. Moreover when activity increases the yield of taxes goes up. Incomes are higher, and more income tax is paid, more tea and beer and cigarettes are consumed. With the same rates of taxes as before the receipts of the Exchequer go up. It is calculated that, one way and another, something like half of the outlay upon public works comes directly back to the government, even when allowance is made for the leakage of secondary employment to foreign countries. Thus to finance a scheme of, say, £100 million the government has to add to its borrowing only £50 million.

This in itself provides a strong argument, from the government point of view, for pressing forward with public works schemes when unemployment exists. Suppose that the rate of interest is 3 per cent. Then any scheme which is reckoned to yield $1\frac{1}{2}$ per cent. on its initial cost, either in direct money receipts (for instance the rent received from a state housing scheme) or in indirect benefits (for instance the advantages of having better roads), is a sound investment even from a narrow commercial point of view.

This is one of the most striking instances of a divergence between individual and social advantage. Any private entrepreneur who decides to undertake investment is benefiting his fellow entrepreneurs and the government, by causing an increase in incomes, in consumption and in tax payments. But the private entrepreneur feels no benefit from the additional incomes which his action causes other people to earn, and if he is borrowing at 3 per cent. he must see at least a 3 per cent. return on his outlay. Thus a government has strong motives for undertaking investment which the private entrepreneur does not feel.

But this is not the end of the story. When investment takes place, then, as we have seen, incomes are increased to such an extent that saving is increased as much as investment. Thus private individuals add to their wealth sums equal to the additional government borrowing, and this they retain as a permanent possession. Interest on a government loan has to be paid out of taxation, and if the National Debt increases tax payments have to increase to provide interest. But the taxpayers, taken together, are precisely the same people as the interest receivers. Their wealth, in their capacity as owners of capital, has gone up exactly as much as their liabilities, in their capacity as taxpayers responsible for the National Debt. Thus, except for a certain nuisance-cost of collecting additional taxes (which may, it is true, become important if the National Debt is very large), the community as a whole is no worse off for the extra government borrowing. Even if the public works were quite useless in themselves they still would not constitute any expense to the community as a whole; while the community would enjoy the benefits of a higher level of employment, income and consumption while the works were being carried out.

To look at the same thing in another way, when there is unemployment resources are idle. The only real cost of setting them to work is a reduction in undesired idleness. Any addition to the real capital of the country resulting from public works, however great or small it may be, is a pure gain; and over and above the permanent gain of real capital there is the temporary gain of increased consumption and diminished misery which occurs as long as the schemes are being carried out. The idea that public works can be " wasteful ", in a time of severe unemployment, is therefore an illusion. It would be wasteful to undertake foolish projects instead of sensible ones, but it is not wasteful to undertake even foolish projects instead of none at all. For if none are undertaken, resources are wasted in idleness, and nothing is saved by not doing the works.

It thus appears that when private entrepreneurs are not undertaking sufficient investment to provide a high level of employment, governments have a strong motive to increase investment in public works. During the years of severe depression following 1929, governments have been acting increasingly on this view. This country has been somewhat exceptional, and British governments have on the whole allowed themselves to be swayed by the same sentiments as private entrepreneurs—increasing public works just when trade is improving, and indulging in so-called economy just when unemployment begins to increase. But, the world over, governments have begun to realise that they can help to prevent fluctuations in employment by increasing public works when private investment falls off. Public works therefore act to some extent as a counterweight to the fluctuations in investment undertaken by profit-seeking entrepreneurs.

INVESTMENT IN WORKING CAPITAL AND STOCKS

Two special kinds of investment must also be considered. These are investment in working capital and investment in stocks of goods. When output is increasing, working capital, that is the value of goods in process, must increase. As soon as output has settled down to a new higher level the investment in working capital comes to an end. When you are starting to make sausages you begin by putting some meat into the back of the sausage machine, and for a few minutes, as you turn the handle, nothing comes out at the front. Meanwhile the amount of meat in the machine is increasing. After a time sausage meat begins to come out at the front at the same rate as you are putting it in at the back, and the amount of meat in the machine ceases to increase. Similarly, when you decide to stop, for a

37

certain time after you have ceased to put meat in at the back it continues to come out at the front, and meanwhile the amount of meat in the machine is falling off, until finally the machine becomes empty.

Any change in the rate of output of industry leads to investment or disinvestment in working capital, and the effect upon employment of investment in working capital is the same as the effect of investment in capital goods. Men are paid wages for starting to produce goods before the goods are ready for sale, and expenditure from their wages falls upon goods already becoming available. Thus there is a special kind of investment which is made for a certain period after the decision has been taken to increase output, and this is an important reason why any influence towards an increase in output tends to amplify itself up to a certain point.

Investment in stocks of goods, on the other hand, acts rather as a counterweight to other forms of investment. When demand is falling off dealers may prefer to accumulate stocks of non-perishable commodities, such as wheat or metals, rather than to sell them at a loss, so that for a time increased investment in stocks partly counterbalances diminished investment in durable capital goods and in working capital. Similarly, when trade begins to revive goods are taken from stocks to be sold, and while stocks are falling, a given increase in expenditure upon consumption goods leads a correspondingly smaller increase in the rate of output of new consumption goods.

These two movements, changes in working capital and changes in stocks, come into play when output, for other reasons, is in the course of changing. They may be of considerable importance, but are not likely by themselves to initiate a change in activity.

CHAPTER V

CHANGES IN THRIFTINESS

THE SCHEDULE OF THRIFTINESS

WE have seen already that a change in the desire to save is powerless to alter the actual amount of saving done by the community as a whole, for the actual rate of saving is determined by the rate of investment which is being undertaken. But the desire to save has an important influence on the level of incomes. If I decide to save £1 a week more than formerly, the shopkeepers and manufacturers who had been supplying my wants now receive £1 a week less than before. Consequently they must either save less or spend less. In so far as they spend less, other incomes are reduced, and so on round and round. Thus the reduction in my expenditure by £1 a week leads to a fall in incomes to such a point that the savings of other people are reduced by £1 per week. If the Multiplier is 3, the reduction in my expenditure by £1 a week will cause a fall in income of £3 per week. After, say, a year I shall have added £52 to my wealth, but others will be poorer by £52 than they would have been if I had not saved that sum. Thus for all of us taken together wealth has not increased, but income has declined.

In short, the rate of investment determines the rate of saving, and given the rate of investment, the desire to save determines the level of incomes. By the desire to save, or *thriftiness* of the community, we mean the whole complex of influences which determine how much will be saved at each level of income. The thriftiness of an individual is represented by a schedule of the amount he would save at each level of income, and the thriftiness of the community is represented by the total of saving corresponding to each level of total income. For this country a small section of the schedule of thriftiness is something like this :

£ Million	
Income	Saving
4300	280
4600	420
4800	530

Given the schedule of thriftiness the level of income depends upon the rate of investment. Thus, in the above example, if investment is being carried out at a rate of £420 million per year, income will be £4600 million per year. With a lower rate of investment, income would be lower, with a higher rate higher. The level of income is always such as to equate the rate of saving to the rate of investment.

The Influence of the Stock Exchange

Changes in thriftiness may accompany the ups and downs of trade. An improved state of confidence about the future may not only lead entrepreneurs to invest more but also may lead individuals to spend more, for as the weather improves the fear of a rainy day grows less acute.

There is a special reason for expecting this sort of thing to happen. When trade improves the prospects of industrial concerns of all sorts look brighter, and precisely the same capital assets are valued by the public at a higher figure, because confidence in their future earning and dividend-paying power has gone up. In short there is a boom on the Stock Exchange. Now any individual who happened to have bought some shares before the boom began finds that their value has risen, that is to say, if he sold them now he would get more for them than he paid. He may not want to sell, but the fact that he *could* sell at a high figure gives him a comfortable sensation and makes him feel rich. He is therefore less stern in denying himself expenditure on consumption of all sorts, and his rate of saving goes down.

The original Stock Exchange boom was a consequence of the increase in prospective profits, which both results from and further promotes an increase in investment. On top of this the Stock Exchange boom promotes increased consumption. Thus there is an increase in the rate of consumption corresponding to a given rate of investment at the same time as investment itself is increasing. The upswing of activity, employment and profits therefore tends to magnify itself. This phenomenon was of great importance during the great Wall Street boom which ended in 1929. It is probably also at work in a milder way whenever there is a marked rise in Stock Exchange prices.

A BUDGET DEFICIT

A special kind of reduction in thriftiness is represented by a budget deficit. If the state is paying out more money in salaries to civil servants, commissions to contractors and so forth, than it is receiving in taxation, and is borrowing the difference by issuing Treasury bills or otherwise raising loans from the public, then it is in just the same position as an individual who is spending on current consumption more than his income, by means of drawing on past accumulated wealth or getting into debt. In short the state is dis-saving. The result is to increase incomes and expenditure all round. Suppose that the state keeps its outlay constant and remits taxation. Then out of the increased net income of taxpayers part will be spent, and this extra spending will raise the incomes of those on whose output the expenditure is made. Out of this extra income, again, a part will be spent ; and so on. Just as in the case of investment, the extra expenditure will lead to such an increase in incomes that the public are saving more than they otherwise would have done at just the same rate as the government is borrowing.

The idea that a budget deficit is good for trade is often found to be shocking, but it is a fact which has become obvious to the governments of the world since the great depression began in 1929. The argument used to be common, particularly in England, that a budget deficit upsets the confidence of entrepreneurs, and so does more indirect harm to employment than direct good. But this is a case where " thinking makes it so ", and it is found nowadays that a deficit accompanied by the right sort of propaganda can have a very beneficial effect.

The mere fact that a deficit is good for trade is not a sufficient argument for having a deficit, since other methods of improving trade may be preferable. It can, however, be regarded as a merciful dispensation that budgets have a tendency to come unstuck when trade is very bad. Taxes fail to yield as much as was expected, while expenses in connection with unemployment go up, and the government is forced to borrow to meet its current outgoings. This has the effect of preventing the decline in employment from going so far as it would if the budget were kept balanced.

INEQUALITY OF INCOMES

An important influence upon the thriftiness of the community is the distribution of a given total income amongst individuals. Generally speaking, the more unequally is income distributed the greater will be the thriftiness of the community. If £100 a year is taken away from a man with £10,000 a year, he will not alter his standard of life very much, but will reduce his rate of saving. But if £100 a year is given to a man who had £150 before, his standard of life will certainly be raised to very nearly the full extent of the extra income. Thus taking the two men together the transfer will increase the amount of consumption out of their combined income of £10,150. We have already seen this principle at work in the determination of the Multiplier, for we found that a given increment of income will lead to a greater increment of saving the more of that increment of income goes to profits and the less to wages.

The general psychological attitude to saving, depending upon family affection, prudence, self-control and so forth, being unaltered, thriftiness will be reduced if measures are taken to reduce the inequality of income. Suppose that the tax system is altered in such a way that a larger amount of taxes is paid by the richest part of the community and a smaller amount by the poorest. The net income of the richest class is now reduced. They will cut down their expenditure to some extent, but not to the full extent of the additional taxation. On the other hand the increased net incomes of the poorest class will be devoted almost entirely to increased consumption. Thus the amount saved out of a given total income will be reduced, while increased expenditure will bring about an increase in the total of income, so that the actual amount of saving is no less than before.

It has sometimes been argued that the fact that inequality of incomes promotes thriftiness is a justification for inequality, and it is held to be highly dangerous to tax the rich for the benefit of the poor on the ground that it will dry up the source from which capital accumulation comes. Even on its own ground this argument is very unconvincing. It is an extremely uneconomic method of getting saving done to fatten up a certain number of people to the point at which saving is no effort to them, and if it is held to be the justification of high incomes that they are partly saved, then all that part which is spent in providing the rich with a luxurious standard of life must be regarded as pure waste. Moreover there is no reason to suppose that the degree of thriftiness which results from inequality of incomes corresponds to the desirability of saving from a social point of view. It would be the height of folly for a man to ruin his health by starvation in the present in order to accumulate wealth for the future, and it is hard to contend, in existing circumstances, that a more rapid rate of capital accumulation is to be preferred to a higher standard of life for the poorest part of the community.

But however that may be, the attempt to justify inequality because it promotes thriftiness falls to the ground as soon as we realise that an increase in thriftiness does not by itself cause an increase in capital accumulation to take place.

THRIFT AS A SOCIAL VIRTUE

Thriftiness does not cause investment to take place, but at the same time it is thriftiness which makes investment possible. There is always an upper limit to the expansion of output, set by the resources available. The more thrifty people are, that is, the less they are inclined to consume, the more resources are left over from providing for current consumption, and these resources (given time to transfer men, and adapt land and machinery, from one use to another) are available to be used for investment. When the motive for investment is weak the resources run to waste in idleness, and we are inclined to regard a reduction of thriftiness as a benefit to society. If these resources are not being used to accumulate capital for the future, we say, let us at least enjoy what we can by eating up their products in the present. But when the motive for investment is strong the whole matter appears in a different light. When the rate of investment is pressing against the limit set by available resources, and all workers are fully employed, then no further increase in the rate of investment can take place unless consumption declines, and an increase in consumption, in such circumstances, instead of setting idle resources to work, can only be made at the expense of investment.

In an age of expansion, when opportunities for profitable investment are never lacking, thriftiness instead of appearing as a cause of unemployment, appears as a cause of investment, and all the increased wealth which results from the accumulation of capital equipment—houses, roads, machinery—is attributed to the beneficent effects of thrift. This view of thriftiness colours much of traditional economic teaching, and some writers, as we saw, have even sought to justify the unequal distribution of incomes because inequality promotes thriftiness.

At the present day, when the problem of unemployment preoccupies our minds, so that even when a boom begins to develop talk immediately turns to what will happen in the next slump, such a view of thriftiness appears paradoxical, or even pernicious. But in other circumstances thriftiness becomes a social virtue. In war time, when all resources released from private consumption are immediately snapped up by the military machine, in Soviet Russia, where there is an insatiable demand for new capital equipment, even, to a milder extent, in the age when railway building was absorbing huge amounts of new capital, the choice, for the community, between present consumption and future wealth (or the demands of war) is a real one, and every man who is kept occupied in providing for present consumption is prevented from contributing to new investment, or to the necessities of war.

These examples point the contrast between an ideal system in which abstinence creates real wealth, and the system that we know, in which economy leads to waste and sound finance is the cause of bankruptcy. But they also serve to warn us against too extreme a reaction from the traditional view of thriftiness as the first of the economic virtues.

SYRACUSE UNIVERSITY
LIBRARY

CHAPTER VI

SUPPOSED REMEDIES FOR UNEMPLOYMENT

CHANGES IN WAGES

WE have seen that employment may be increased by an increase in investment or by a decline in thriftiness. These two categories divide the whole field, and (apart from reductions in efficiency which mean that more labour is required for a given output) any influence that tends to increase employment can be analysed into either an increase in investment or a reduction in thriftiness.

It is sometimes argued that another way to increase employment is to raise wages. If entrepreneurs agree to pay their workers higher rates, money demand for goods is increased, and it is argued from this that activity and output will increase. But this rise in demand merely offsets the rise in cost of production due to higher wages. A larger expenditure of money is now needed to buy the same goods, and the increase in money income is not an increase in real purchasing power. There is no simple remedy for unemployment to be found merely in raising wages.

The reverse argument is also common. It is said that if wages were reduced costs would fall, and therefore entrepreneurs would find it profitable to produce more goods. But money incomes fall as much as costs, and money demand is reduced correspondingly. Any one entrepreneur, by cutting the wage rate which he pays, can increase his profits, but at the same time he is reducing the receipts of other entrepreneurs, and if they all cut wages together none of them are any better off. Any one man in the crowd can get a better view of the procession by standing on a chair, but if they all get up on chairs no one's view is improved.

Any change in money wages will set up a number of complicated repercussions, which may lead to a change in employment, in one direction or the other, to some extent, but (apart from reactions upon the rate of interest, which we shall discuss later) a change in money wages is not likely to lead to any great change in employment in either direction.

MONOPOLY

In times of severe depression restriction schemes are widely adopted in order to keep up prices in particular industries and prevent the profits from disappearing altogether. A violent fall in demand puts entrepreneurs in a desperate position, and any group which can get together and agree to cut down their output by collective

51

action can mitigate their own share in the general disaster. By keeping up the price of their own product, and dismissing workers even more extensively than they would have done if competition had continued to prevail, they benefit themselves at the expense of the consumers and the workers. And because they impoverish consumers and workers they damage other entrepreneurs also, by reducing the demand for their commodities. The whole class of entrepreneurs taken together can do themselves little good by these methods, but any one group can benefit itself at the expense of the rest.

Thus it is natural enough that a time of depression should give birth to a litter of quota systems, amalgamations, price-fixing agreements and even schemes for smashing up productive plant and burning stocks of materials. The strange thing is that this growth of monopolistic practices is often advocated as a remedy for unemployment. The argument is made to sound plausible by confusing a symptom with a cause of disease. When depression sets in profits decline ; therefore, it is said, anything which helps to raise profits will help to remove the depression. And we are asked to believe that dismissing workers and closing down plants is a method of increasing employment. To pursue the argument through all its bewildering paradoxes, and to sort out the few grains of truth that are to be found amongst the chaff of special pleading, would take us too far from the main course of our inquiry, and we must be content to dismiss the matter with the common-sense reflection that scarcity of economic goods (whether natural or artificial) can be a benefit to one section of the community only at the expense of others, and that a net increase of prosperity for the community as a whole cannot arise from the restriction of activity and destruction of resources.

MOBILITY OF LABOUR

It is usual to attribute a large amount of unemployment to " frictions " which prevent workers from moving readily from one occupation or locality to another, and remedies for unemployment are sought in training schemes, in providing facilities for transfer and so forth. Such schemes constitute a remedy for unemployment when activity is at a high level. They serve to reduce the minimum of unemployment which remains even in the best of times. But when unemployment is severe they can be of little use. Lack of mobility of labour can be called a cause of unemployment only when there are unfilled vacancies in some places and idle men in others. When every industry and every locality has its own fringe of unemployed workers there is little to be gained (unless it is desired to even things up between the worst and the least bad districts) by shifting men from place to place.

Lack of mobility is itself largely the result

of a high level of unemployment. The individual worker lacks incentive to move to a new locality or learn a new trade when there is no locality and no trade in which he can be certain of finding work. Schemes to promote mobility are all to the good, but there is no remedy for immobility so effective as the development of boom conditions.

Part of unemployment is sometimes ascribed to the "unemployability" of the individuals concerned, but this, like mobility of labour, is largely a matter of degree. Particular workers who are inefficient, unreliable or who have strong political convictions, will suffer more than an average share of unemployment, and when the general level of activity is low they are labled as "unemployables". But when a revival of trade sets in the employers' standards of efficiency and docility are perforce relaxed, and in the very height of a boom they are often glad to engage whomever they can get. Thus "unemployability", like immobility, melts away when the demand for labour is sufficiently strong.

Reducing the Supply of Labour

There is a certain class of remedies for unemployment which does not involve an increase in trade activity. Workers may be removed from the labour market by, for instance, raising the school-leaving age, or forbidding married women to take jobs. But this is merely to remove some persons from the category of workers and so to reduce unemployment without increasing employment. Or hours of work may be reduced. This has the effect of spreading a given amount of work round amongst more individuals. It is not properly to be regarded as an increase in employment, though it increases the number of individuals employed, for it has no tendency to increase the amount of work done. These various policies may be regarded as methods of reducing the ill effects of unemployment, and they may be desirable on their own merits, but they provide no remedy for the waste of potential real income and wealth which results from under-employment of productive resources.

CHAPTER VII

PRICES

CHANGES IN PRICES

WE have so far discussed influences which affect the level of output. We must now consider the level of prices. Changes in the general level of prices can come about as a result of three distinct groups of causes. First, a change in prices accompanies a change of activity. At any moment there is a certain amount of productive equipment in existence—factories, farms, plantations, machines, ships, rolling-stock and so forth—and output is increased, when demand expands, by employing more labour with the same equipment. In many lines of production, though not necessarily in all, output per man falls off as a greater rate of output is squeezed from the same equipment. And if the same wage is paid per man, cost per unit of output rises when output per man falls. Therefore it would not pay entrepreneurs to produce a greater rate of output unless prices rose, and a rise in the general level of prices normally accompanies an increase in activity.

Secondly, a change in money wages alters the level of prices corresponding to a given level of activity. In any actual situation a change in money wages is likely to be the consequence of a change in activity, and it may, in its turn, be a cause of changes in investment (particularly, as we shall find, through changes in the rate of interest) or in thriftiness, thus leading to a change in activity. Moreover an exactly equal all-round change in wages is never seen, and many complications arise from changes in the relative wages of different industries.

But it can be seen that an equal change in all wages which is not accompanied by a change in activity must lead to an equal proportional change in prices.

The raw materials and the capital goods used by one industry are the product of another industry, and, for industry as a whole in the world as a whole, costs of production (apart from changes in the rate of interest) depend upon wages. Let us suppose that there is an all-round rise of money-wage rates of, say, 10 per cent. Then the costs of a given output are raised 10 per cent. ; and (unless something has happened to alter output) prices must rise by 10 per cent. Since receipts and costs are raised in the same proportion, profits are also raised in that proportion. But, as prices have also risen in the same proportion, neither real wages nor real profits are changed.

Hardly so

A rise in wages is demanded by workers in the hope of improving their standard of life, and granted with reluctance by employers, who fear a decline in their profits. But where there is an all-round change the one party is unpleasantly, and the other pleasantly, surprised by the result. Experience, all the same, can never teach that the struggle is vain, for wage bargains are made by particular groups of workers and of employers, and any one group which falls behind when a general movement takes place suffers a loss or gains an advantage at the expense of the rest.

A third type of change in prices comes about from a change in efficiency. As time goes by, capital equipment accumulates and improvements in technique are introduced, so that output per man increases, and if money wages are constant there is a tendency for the price level corresponding to a given level of output to fall. Over a period of generations, the general level of prices will move up or down according as money wages rise by more or by less than efficiency increases.

Prices and the State of Trade

It is well known that a rise in prices normally accompanies an improvement in trade. We can now see how this comes about. An increase in activity sets on foot a rise in prices of the first type, while the consequent decline in unemployment is likely to lead to a rise of the second type, that is to say, a rise in money wages. The level of money wages alters with the push and pull of bargaining between employers and workers. Bargaining strength depends upon all sorts of considerations, and varies very much from country to country and from generation to generation. For instance, there was a marked growth in the strength of Trade Union organisation in this country in the latter part of the nineteenth century. But whatever the general situation may be, as between workers and employers, the scales tip in favour of the workers when trade is active and unemployment low, and in favour of the employers when unemployment is severe. Thus an upward movement of wages sets in in good times and a fall in bad times.

The public have become so much accustomed to thinking of the rise in prices that occurs when trade improves that it is commonly said that " rising prices are good for trade ". But this is a very confusing way of looking at the matter. The rise in prices which occurs in the first instance, because demand has increased, is a symptom, not a cause, of the increase in demand. Trade is not stimulated because prices rise, but prices rise because trade is stimulated.

The rise in prices does not measure the improvement in trade. If supply is very elastic, because, may be, there is so much surplus plant, before the revival begins, that output per man falls very little as employment increases, then a large increase in output is accompanied by a very small rise in prices, and the fact that prices have not much risen is all to the good. In the early stages of a revival of trade after a slump prices normally rise very little, and only when unemployment has fallen considerably, and factories are working near to capacity, does a sharp rise in prices set in.

The secondary rise in prices, due to the rise in money wages which comes about when a fall in unemployment strengthens the bargaining position of workers, is not a symptom of improved trade, but an indirect consequence of it, and as we shall find at a later stage in the argument, the revival is more likely to continue if prices do *not* rise for this reason than if they do.

Similarly a fall in prices may be due to a falling off in demand, or it may be the result of wage-cuts, or it may be due to the accumulation of capital equipment and to improved methods of production. In the first case the fall is a symptom of bad trade, but not a cause of it. In the second case the fall in prices is an indirect consequence of bad trade, since wages fall when unemployment is rife ; and in the last case the fall in prices is a symptom of improved efficiency.

REAL WAGES

A second well-known phenomenon is that real wages, that is, the goods which a man can buy with his wage, fall off as trade improves. Wages, it is said, fail to catch up on prices : when the cost of living rises, as the result of an improvement in trade, money wages do not rise fast enough to offset the rise in prices, and the real-wage rate falls. We are now able to see why this must be so. The initial increase in demand raises prices relatively to money wages, while any rise in wages produces an equivalent further rise in prices ; and prices move ahead of wages as the horizon moves ahead of the traveller.

Any one group of workers whose wages rise faster than the rest gain an advantage, for their money incomes rise faster than the prices of commodities produced by other people. But the price of the commodity which they produce rises faster than the money incomes of other workers, and for all workers taken together the real-wage rate falls as activity increases.

The Rate of Interest and Prices

Another well-known phenomenon is the relationship between changes in Bank-rate and changes in prices. The practical experience of banking authorities has taught them that if they desire to bring about a fall in prices (as they may be obliged to do for reasons connected with the foreign exchanges, which we will discuss later), their best course is to engineer a rise in the rate of interest. We can now see how it comes about that this policy is successful. Schemes of investment, as we have seen, are made in the light of a comparison between prospective profits and the rate of interest, and when the rate of interest rises schemes of investment which were profitable at the lower rate of interest cease to be profitable. The rate of production of houses, ships, machinery and so forth, begins to fall off soon after the rise in the rate of interest has made itself felt. Men are thrown out of work, the Multiplier comes into play, the ball of activity rolls downhill, and output and incomes in all industries decline. And with the lower level of activity prices are lower.

This is the first stage of the effect of a rise in the rate of interest, and it is a painful one. As time goes by new wage-bargains are made and, with the higher level of unemployment, workers (perhaps after unsuccessful strikes) are compelled to accept lower money wages. A fall in money wages is the second stage in the operation of a rise in the rate of interest. If the fall in prices due to the fall in wages is sufficient to satisfy the authorities, the rate of interest can now be lowered again and activity can be allowed to recover.

When Trade Unions are strong, wages may be prevented from falling, and the system may drag painfully on for years on end at the first stage in the operation of Bank-rate policy. And even if wages fall, the fall will normally be uneven as between trades, those workers who can least afford a cut being forced, because of the weakness of their position, to take the greatest cuts. Thus the policy of forcing down prices, even if it is successful in the end, leads to much loss and suffering and social injustice.

Gains and Losses from Changing Prices

We are now able to see the effects of changing
activity and changing prices upon various classes
of the community. At first sight we might be
inclined to say that everyone is pleased when
trade improves, but actually this is not the case.
An increase in activity leads to a rise in prices,
an increase in employment, a fall in real-wage
rates and a rise in profits. Workers who were
formerly unemployed are now better off, but
those who were employed already suffer from the
fall in real wages. Many will gain from an increased sense of security, but a man who was in
no danger of losing his job in the slump is better
off during the slump than when revival sets in.
Thus even for the workers a revival in trade is not
an unambiguous benefit.

But the chief sufferers from a revival are the
fixed-income classes. A large number of contracts,
such as salaries and interest on debentures and
government loans, are fixed in terms of money.
Anyone whose income is fixed in terms of money
is better off under slump conditions, provided
that the slump is not so severe as to drive
debtors to default. The only people who have no
cause to complain of a revival of trade are entrepreneurs, whose total receipts rise while a large
part of their costs are fixed in terms of money.

A rise in money wages, which, as we have
seen, is neutral from the point of view of workers
taken as a whole, imposes a further loss of real

income upon the fixed-income class, while entrepreneurs gain what their creditors lose. If the receipts of a firm rise, and its debenture interest remains the same, the profits of the ordinary shareholders rise in a greater proportion than total receipts, and since total receipts rise in proportion to prices, real profits are increased.

To sum up : A rise in prices which is a symptom of improving trade is partly beneficial and partly harmful to the workers, since it is accompanied by both an increase in employment and a fall in real wages. A rise in prices which is due to a rise in money wages is, in itself, neutral from the point of view of workers. While a rise in prices, of either kind, is beneficial to entrepreneurs and harmful to the fixed-income class. Since a rise in activity not only leads directly to a rise in prices but is also likely to set a rise in money wages on foot, all those whose income is fixed in terms of money have good reason to dread a prosperous state of trade.

CHAPTER VIII

THE RATE OF INTEREST

THE NATURE OF INTEREST

WE have seen that the rate of interest has an extremely important influence on the level of employment, since it affects the decisions of entrepreneurs as to how much it is worth their while to invest in new capital goods. We must now discuss what it is that determines the rate of interest.

Interest is the payment made for borrowing, that is, for acquiring the use of money for a certain time. The essence of a transaction involving interest is that one man parts with money in return for an I O U from another man. The lender acquires a piece of paper representing his right to repayment, and the borrower acquires the immediate use of the money. The borrower must make some payment to the lender, over and above the eventual repayment of the sum borrowed, for if he did not do so the lender (apart from philanthropy) would have no motive for parting with control over his money, and for undergoing the risk that the borrower (through villainy or mere bad luck) may default when repayment is due. This extra payment is the interest on the loan. The motive of the borrower is that he can use the money to acquire capital goods which he expects to earn at least as much as the interest which he has to pay (or, in the case of private borrowing, because he needs money now more than he expects to need it in the future). The motive of the lender is to receive interest. All transactions involving interest, whether it takes the form of an agreed sum or a share in profits, can be reduced to terms of this simple pattern.

The I O U's (bonds, shares, etc.) can change hands, and the ruling rate of interest is shown in the relationship between the income yielded by a security and the price at which it sells. Thus a fall in security prices means a rise in the rate of interest, and a rise in security prices a fall in the rate of interest.

Suppose that a government loan is issued on the terms: £3 per year for every £100 subscribed to the loan. Then if the bond representing £100 originally subscribed stands at par, this means that the rate of interest is 3 per cent. If it stands at £150, the rate of interest is 2 per cent., and if it stands at £80 the rate of interest is $3\frac{3}{4}$ per cent.

A share which is expected to earn a dividend of £3 will normally sell for less than £100 when the government bond sells for £100, for the return on the government bond is more certain. No one has any motive for holding a more risky security unless it gives a higher yield than a safer security. In what follows, however, we shall not discuss all the complications involved in the relative yields of different types of securities and we shall speak of *the* rate of interest, meaning the whole complex of interest rates on securities of all sorts.

THE DEMAND FOR MONEY

Anyone who owns money could earn interest, if he chose to lend it. The question therefore arises, Why does anyone hold money at all ? This question at first sight seems strange. We would all like to have some more money. But what we would like to have is a larger income, or more wealth. The question now before us does not concern a man's rate of income, reckoned in money terms, or the total wealth which he has acquired by past saving or by inheritance ; it concerns the form in which he holds wealth that he owns. Why should anyone hold part of his wealth in cash or on a current account at his bank, so that it earns no interest, or on deposit account where it earns very low interest, when he might acquire more interest by lending it ?

One reason for holding money arises more or less automatically from the manner in which payments are customarily made. Most people receive their incomes at certain intervals and make payments continuously day by day. Shop-keepers and bus companies, on the other hand, receive payments day by day and make payments at longer intervals. At any moment sums are held in the form of money which the individual owner will shortly be going to pay away to someone else, and it would not be worth while to lend them at interest for the short time before they are to be drawn upon.

The amount of money required for this sort of reason will depend partly upon the intervals at which income is received. Suppose a man has an income of £365 a year, of which he spends the whole on current consumption at a steady rate of £1 per day. If his income is paid weekly, he holds, on average, at least £3 : 10s. in cash (£7 on the first day of each week, and nothing on the last). If his income is paid quarterly he holds, on average, at least £45 : 10s., and if it is paid yearly, £182 : 10s. Thus the amount of money which people require for convenience balances varies with the manner in which their income is received. Given the complex of habits governing the intervals of payments, the demand for convenience balances will depend upon the level of income. If money incomes in general are higher there will be an automatic increase in the amount of money that people want to hold. This fact, as we shall find, is of considerable importance.

Money may also be held by individuals who own a small amount of wealth which they do not feel it worth while to put out at interest. Suppose that the man who is spending the whole of his weekly income of £7 also owns £5, which he has saved in the past, and is keeping as a reserve. Then his average holding of money is £8 : 10s. Again, individuals who have a larger amount of wealth may like to hold a certain sum in a readily accessible form, say in a bank account, as a safeguard against a sudden emergency. A large number of small sums held in the form of money for such reasons as these amount to a considerable total for the community as a whole.

Larger sums may be held by individual owners of wealth who are refraining from buying interest-bearing securities at the moment because they expect them to be cheaper in a short time, that is to say, they are expecting a rise in the rate of interest to take place. If *all* owners of wealth were confidently expecting a rise in the rate of interest, all would be anxious to sell securities at existing prices, and the prices of securities would fall immediately to the point at which no further fall was expected, so that no one would want to hold money. But so long as there are differences of opinion amongst owners of wealth some will be holding money, expecting a future fall in the price of securities, while others are refraining from selling the securities they hold in the expectation that the price is not going to fall. Moreover no one is ever quite confident that his best guess at what is likely to happen is really a good guess, and many people hold part of their wealth in the form of money just because it is the one thing whose price in terms of money they can be sure will not alter.

The Demand for Money and the Rate of Interest

For these reasons there is always a certain amount of money that people want to hold, in spite of the fact that they can get interest by parting with it. But the higher the rate of interest, other things equal, the less money will they want to hold, for interest represents the sacrifice entailed by holding money. The convenience and the sense of security obtained by owning money are weighed against the interest obtained by parting with it, and the greater the advantage of parting with money the less will people want to hold.

By the amount of money we mean the amount of coins, notes and bank deposits. Individuals possess, at any moment, some coins and notes, or have deposits standing in their names. The sum of all the amounts that they own is the total quantity of money. Deposits which are being held at any moment as convenience balances to bridge the gap between receipts and payments are known as the *active* deposits, because they pass rapidly from one individual to another as payments are made. Deposits which are used as a form of holding accumulated wealth, as an alternative to securities, are *inactive*. In normal times notes and coins belong almost entirely to the active circulation, though perhaps there are still some people who like to keep part of their wealth in the chimney corner. In general, the amount of active deposits which people desire to hold is not much affected by the rate of interest, though a very high rate may tempt people to economise on their convenience balances to some extent. The main influence of the rate of interest upon the amount of money which people want to hold is on the amount of inactive balances.

On any day in the year there is a certain amount of money (notes, coin and bank deposits) in existence, and all this money must be owned by someone. From moment to moment the rate of interest must find its level at the point at which people, taken together, are willing to hold just the amount of money that there is. For if the rate of interest were higher than this level some owners of money would be anxious to buy securities with their money in order to obtain interest. The desire to buy securities drives up their price and so lowers the rate of interest, and this process must be carried to the point at which no owner of money any longer wishes to buy securities. Similarly, if on any day the rate of interest were lower than the level at which people are content to hold the amount of money there is on that day, they would be anxious to sell securities and the rate would rise. Thus, given the total of wealth in existence, the ruling level of income, and the state of expectations about the future, the rate of interest is determined from moment to moment by the quantity of money. Just now, as you turn this page (unless it is out of office hours), to-day's rate of interest is being determined, and is moving to the level at which no one who owns securities wants to sell them and no one who owns money wants to buy them.

THE SUPPLY OF MONEY

The quantity of money, in turn, is determined by the banking system, acting within the framework of certain legal and customary rules. The most important part of the supply of money, in modern conditions, is represented by bank deposits, and it is through the action of the banks that the amount of money is controlled.

In the British system the banks keep a certain ratio (about 1 to 9) of " cash " to other assets. " Cash " consists of notes and coins in the tills of the banks and deposits with the Bank of England, which are regarded as equivalent to actual cash. The other assets of the banks consist of bills, advances and securities. These all represent loans of different kinds, and since there is no difference of principle between one and another we may conveniently lump them all together under the title of securities. Securities earn interest and cash earns none. The banks therefore do not want to hold an unnecessarily large amount of cash. On the other hand they do not want their ratio of cash to fall below what is traditionally regarded as the safe and respectable figure.

The custom of preserving a strict cash ratio

gives the Bank of England power to control the total amount of bank deposits. Let us see how this comes about. When the Bank wishes to increase the amount of deposits, so that the rate of interest may be forced down, it buys securities on the open market. Suppose that a Mr. Snooks parts with £100 worth of gilt-edged securities and receives £100 from the Bank. He pays this £100 into his own bank account. His bank now finds itself with its total of deposits increased by £100 and its assets increased by £100 of cash in its deposit with the Bank of England. To prevent its cash ratio from rising unnecessarily high it makes use of £90 from this £100 to buy securities, thus restoring the ratio of cash to other assets to the customary figure of 1 to 9. But the £90 which it expends in this way now appears as additional deposits and additional cash in the accounts of other banks (a part may come back to the same bank), who consequently buy securities to the extent of £81. And so on round and round until the Bank's original purchase of £100 of securities from Mr. Snooks has led to an increase in the total of deposits of £1000, against which the banks hold £100 more cash and £900 more securities. The public are now holding £1000 more deposits than before and the banks (including the Bank of England) are holding £1000 more of securities. Thus for every £100 of securities bought by the Bank of England £1000 are bought by the banking system as a whole.

The purchase of securities by the banks drives up their price (thus lowering the rate of interest) to whatever point is required to make the public willing to part with the securities and hold deposits instead. Thus the power to induce an increase in the total amount of bank deposits enables the Bank of England to bring about a fall in the rate of interest when it wishes to do so. The reverse process, of selling securities in the open market and forcing the banks to reduce deposits, is used when a rise in the rate of interest is required. Control by these " open market operations " is supplemented by the direct control of Bank-rate, which is kept in step with the movements of the general complex of interest rates dictated by the Bank's policy.

The freedom of action of the Bank is not absolute, for when the gold standard is in force it is obliged to regulate its operations in such a way as to maintain an adequate gold reserve, and even when there is no gold standard it is still obliged to consider the stability of the foreign exchanges. This matter will be considered in a later chapter.

In most other banking systems the control of the Central Bank is not so well established as in the British system, but in all countries the same principles are at work, though they may show themselves in somewhat different forms. In every case the banking system as a whole determines the amount of deposits, and lowers or raises the rate of interest by buying or selling securities and increasing or reducing the amount of deposits held by the public. Thus, within the limits set by its legal or customary obligations, the banking system can control the rate of interest by operating on the quantity of money.

Normally the banks operate directly only upon the short-term rate of interest, but if the yield on one kind of security falls, people sell out that kind of security in order to buy others, and so the rise in price and fall in yield is transmitted to all classes of securities until the whole complex of interest rates is affected.

CHANGES IN THE DEMAND FOR MONEY

If the banking authorities wish to keep the rate of interest constant, they must offset changes in the demand for money by altering the quantity of money. First, the gradual increase in the total of wealth which comes about as investment continues year after year will increase the amount of money which people require to hold. Thus the quantity of money must gradually increase as time goes by if the rate of interest is to be prevented from rising.

Second, a change in trade activity alters the demand for money. When trade is more active and employment greater, the amount of money which people require for the active circulation goes up. Similarly a rise in money wages and prices raises the demand for money. Thus, when trade improves or wages rise the rate of interest will rise unless the quantity of money is increased.

Finally, a change in the state of confidence about the future alters the amount of wealth which the owners of wealth want to hold in the form of money, at a given rate of interest, in order to feel a sense of security. Thus, if the demand for money rises as the result of an upset to confidence, the quantity of money must be increased in order to prevent the rate of interest from rising.

It is here that we find the proper significance of " hoarding ". An increase in the desire to hold money, as opposed to securities, will tend to drive up the rate of interest, and so to bring about a fall in activity. But there is no connection between this and the fall in activity directly produced by an increase in the desire to save.

A Change in the Rate of Interest

We are now able to see how the causes and the consequences of a change in the rate of interest react upon each other. Let us suppose that the Bank of England carries out open-market purchases and the other banks respond in the usual way by bringing about an increase in the total of deposits. In the first instance nothing has happened to the total of wealth, the level of incomes, or the state of confidence, but the banks are holding more securities and the public have parted with securities and are holding deposits instead. The rate of interest is therefore forced down to the point at which the public are willing to hold the additional deposits. The rate falls, say, from 4 per cent. to $3\frac{1}{2}$ per cent.

After the rate of interest has ruled at $3\frac{1}{2}$ per cent. for a few months schemes of investment which were not being undertaken at 4 per cent., but which are profitable at $3\frac{1}{2}$ per cent., begin to be carried out. Men are set to work at building and so forth, activity and incomes increase in accordance with the Multiplier, and an improvement in trade sets in. Now, supposing that no further change in the quantity of money takes place, the rate of interest will rise somewhat, for with larger incomes the requirements of the active circulation are increased. It rises, at this stage, perhaps to $3\frac{3}{4}$ per cent., but it cannot go back to 4 per cent., for if it did investment would relapse to its former level and the increased demand for convenience balances would disappear again.

With increased employment the position of workers is strengthened, and a rise in money wages may set in. With each rise in wages and prices the demand for money for convenience balances is increased, people find it necessary to sell out securities in order to provide themselves with a fund of cash, and the rate of interest is driven up. The higher the level of money wages the greater is the demand for money at a given level of activity, and once wages are up they will not easily come down again, even when employment falls off. Thus the rate of interest may be driven, by the rise in wages, back towards the 4 per cent. at which it originally stood, so that the stimulus to trade activity disappears.

We have here seen one of the most important influences which brings a revival of trade to an end. Normally, for whatever reason a revival may begin, it will lead to a rise in the rate of interest, which checks investment and brings the revival to an end. A revival in trade is always in danger of cutting its own throat.

Moreover we have now seen why it is that in normal times full employment can never be attained. When unemployment has fallen very low, a rapid rise in money wages sets in, the demand for money in the active circulation increases, the rate of interest is driven up, investment falls off, and unemployment increases again.

LIMITS TO THE CONTROL OF THE RATE OF INTEREST

Even if the banking authorities wished to control the rate of interest in such a way as to prevent unemployment they would not find it easy to do so. For the mere accumulation of capital leads to a fall in prospective profits and (unless inventions or increases in population take place sufficiently rapidly) investment is always tending to bring itself to an end. To preserve full employment the rate of interest would have to be constantly falling. A sufficient fall in the actual rate of interest is hard to bring about, first because no one country can lower its rate of interest very far unless the rest of the world follows suit, secondly because powerful vested interests are opposed to very low interest rates, and thirdly because legal and customary rules (particularly when the gold standard is in use) limit the powers of the monetary authorities to control the rate of interest.

Moreover, to preserve full employment the rate of interest would often have to make violent jumps. Prospective profits are much influenced by optimism and pessimism of entrepreneurs, and very violent changes in the rate of interest may be required to influence investment. At the same time changes in the state of confidence react upon the demand for money, so that violent changes in the quantity of money may be required to influence the rate of interest. The problem of maintaining exactly the right rate of interest to preserve full employment is by no means a simple one.

Even if the rate of interest were deliberately controlled with a view to keeping unemployment as low as possible, oscillations in the state of trade would be hard to prevent. But, in the present state of affairs, the rate of interest is not controlled with this end in view. The chief preoccupation of the authorities is to prevent the rapid rise in prices which sets in when unemployment falls very low, and the fear of this evil seems to be far more present to their minds than fear of the evils of unemployment. As things work out the chief function of the rate of interest is to prevent full employment from ever being attained.

CHAPTER IX

ASPECTS OF THE RATE OF INTEREST

THE EARNINGS OF CAPITAL

THE rate of interest is sometimes regarded as being the same thing as the profitability of capital. This is highly misleading. The prospective earnings of capital goods are determined by the general state of trade, and the cost of production of capital goods by technical conditions and the level of money wages in the industries that produce them. These two sets of influences determine the profitability of capital. The rate of interest is the price that has to be paid to borrow money. These are two quite different things, determined by quite different causes. There is a tendency for them to be brought to equality with each other, for if profitability is greater than the rate of interest, entrepreneurs have a motive to create more capital goods, and as the amount in existence increases, their earnings per unit fall. To return to our first example, if a house bringing in a net income of £50 a year costs £1000 to build, and the rate of interest is 4 per cent., then houses of this type will continue to be built until they are so plentiful that the rents at which they can be let yield a net income of only £40.

A rise in the profitability of capital goods with the same rate of interest, or a fall in the rate of interest with the same profitability, will lead to an increase in the number of capital goods in existence sufficient to restore the rate of profit to equality with the rate of interest. The rate of profit and the rate of interest are not the same thing, and they tend to be equal simply because, when they differ, it pays entrepreneurs to act in such a way as to bring the rate of profit into equality with the rate of interest.

The Reward of Waiting

The rate of interest is also sometimes regarded as the " reward of waiting ". This is an ambiguous phrase. It is often used to mean the reward for saving. But this view does not hold water. It is true that the ruling rate of interest may have an effect upon the amount that individuals want to save, but any owner of wealth can get interest by lending it, no matter whether he is at present adding to his wealth by saving or not. Thus interest as a reward for saving is not at all on a par with wages as a reward for work. No one can earn wages this week without working this week, but a man whose ancestors saved (or, for that matter, committed highway robberies) a hundred years ago can receive interest without doing any saving at all.

This objection does not arise if we interpret " waiting " to mean merely spending less on

81

current consumption than the total purchasing power at command. On this view interest is the reward for not bluing your capital. There is a certain moral flavour about the idea of a " reward for waiting ", as something comparable with the reward for working, which wears very thin when it is interpreted to mean merely a reward for owning wealth.

But the rate of interest is not even a reward for owning wealth, for a man may own wealth and hold it in the form of money, which earns no interest. We return therefore to our starting point—the rate of interest is simply the payment for lending money.

THE REGULATOR

Finally, the rate of interest is regarded as a regulator of the economic system. On this view the rate of interest is determined by the supply and demand of new capital, so that, when people become more thrifty, it is held that the rate of interest falls in such a way as to promote a corresponding increase in investment in new capital goods, while, if the profitability of capital goods is increased, it is held that the rate of interest is driven up in such a way as to limit the increase in investment to whatever increase in the desire to save may be induced by the higher rate of interest.

This theory is untenable. It is true, indeed, that an increase in the desire to save tends to lower the rate of interest, but it only does so because it reduces activity and so brings about a fall in the demand for money. And it is true that an increase in investment normally raises the rate of interest, by increasing activity and so raising the demand for money. But whatever the rate of investment may be, incomes will always be such that people save at whatever rate provides the capital which entrepreneurs are investing. A change in demand for capital (investment) always brings about (by way of a change in incomes) an exactly equal change in supply (saving) ; while if willingness to supply capital (thriftiness) increases, but the demand for it (investment) does not go up, no more will actually be saved than before. Thus it is clearly absurd to say that the rate of interest is determined by the supply and demand of capital.

Nevertheless the conception of the rate of interest as the regulator of the economic system contains an important element of truth. We are concerned nowadays with the problem of unemployment, and the paradox of poverty in the midst of plenty overshadows all discussions of economic questions. The failure of a system of private enterprise to regulate itself in such a way as to prevent the waste and misery of unemployment appears to us, in the present age, as its most striking feature. But within very broad limits the system does regulate itself. Very severe unemployment does, slowly and imperfectly, bring about its own cure. For when unemployment is severe then, on the one hand, money wages are driven down, so that the demand for money is reduced, while, on the other hand, the authorities are under pressure to increase the quantity of money in order to help things out. Thus, in a broad general sense, it is true that unemployment causes the rate of interest to fall. At the same time, a very high level of employment leads to a rise in the rate of interest. For as the limit of full employment is approached money wages rise rapidly, and the authorities are anxious to prevent a corresponding increase in the supply of money, so that the rate of interest is forced up.

Thus, when unemployment rises very high or falls very low, counteracting influences are called into play, and the fluctuations of employment are held within certain limits. For the discussion of problems involving broad changes over the course of generations, in population, the rate of technical progress or the general social forces influencing thriftiness, it is possible to regard fluctuations in employment as a secondary consideration, and to conduct the discussion in terms of a self-regulating system. Then, taking a short cut, we may speak as though an increase in the profitability of capital were the cause of a rise in the rate of interest, and an increase in thriftiness the cause of a fall.

We have seen already that, when the motive for investment is strong, an increase in thriftiness may be regarded as a cause of an increase in investment. We now see that there is a more general sense in which thriftiness may be said to cause investment. For when the level of employment is fixed an increase in thriftiness must lead (by way of lowering the rate of interest) to an increase in investment. And in so far as it is true that in reality employment can move only between certain limits it is true that a large-scale increase in thriftiness must lead to a more or less commensurate increase in investment.

A large part of economic theory has been devoted to the study of an ideal self-regulating system, and it is important not to lose sight, in our preoccupation with unemployment, of the principles derived from such a system, which apply in a broad general way to the actual world.

CHAPTER X

CHANGES IN THE SUPPLY OF MONEY

Gold-mining

WE have seen how the creation of additional bank deposits can come about at the initiative of the Central Bank. This operation has no direct effect upon income, for the mere fact that the banks are holding more securities and the public are holding more deposits has no immediate re-action upon anyone's income. At the same time, it has an effect upon income in a roundabout way, because it leads to a fall in the rate of interest, and consequently to an increase in the rate of investment in capital goods.

There are, however, two ways in which the supply of money may be increased which have a direct effect upon the level of incomes, as well as an indirect effect *via* the rate of interest. The first way is by gold-mining. People who make their incomes, whether wages or profits, from gold-mining are in a somewhat similar position to those engaged upon erecting the Tower of Babel. Their activity adds neither to the current output of consumption goods nor to the useful capital equipment of industry. But the ex-penditure which they make from their incomes is laid out upon consumption goods, and the demand for consumption goods increases when increased incomes are made 'from gold-mining. Thus gold-mining is on a par with investment in capital goods, as far as its effect upon employment, profits and prices is concerned, while it is going on, though what it leaves behind as a permanent addition to the stock of wealth is not directly useful, like houses or machines, but has only a conventional value.

The increase in the stock of gold above the surface of the earth, which results from mining, has a further effect upon the situation, for it leads to an increase in the stock of money. Wherever the gold standard is in operation Central Banks are obliged to buy gold as it is presented to them, and a purchase of gold by a Central Bank has precisely the same effects as a purchase of securities in the open market. The seller of the gold deposits the sum he receives for it at his own bank ; the bank finds its " cash " increased by this sum, and the whole chain of consequences follows the course which we have already traced.

When Central Banks wish to fulfil their obligations under the gold standard but do not wish to be forced into increasing the quantity of money just because gold happens to be offered to them, they can offset the purchase of gold by the sale of a corresponding amount of securities. The total of " cash " for the banks then remains the same, and the only change is that the Central

87   G

Bank holds gold in place of securities. This is called " sterilising " the gold, since the quantity of money cannot then increase and multiply in the usual way.

These manœuvres, by which gold is dug from the earth in order to be buried in the vaults of a Central Bank, would seem strange and arbitrary to an observer from Mars ; they have developed by a gradual process, within the framework of legal rules devised to meet the needs of an earlier stage of monetary evolution, and are not the product of any rational plan.

CREATION OF MONEY THROUGH A BUDGET DEFICIT

A budget deficit financed by borrowing from the Central Bank has effects similar to those of gold-mining. We have already seen how a budget deficit influences incomes. If there is an increase in government expenditure without any corresponding increase in tax receipts there will be an increase in incomes and activity. This is true equally whether the government borrows from the public or from the Central Bank. If the borrowing is from the public there is no further effect to be considered. But if borrowing is from the Central Bank, then on top of the direct effect of the deficit upon income there is the effect of an increase in the quantity of money. For the Central Bank, in lending to the government, increases the " cash " of the banks, just as it does by buying securities or by buying gold. The direct effect of the deficit comes to an end as soon as the budget is balanced, but the effect upon the quantity of money remains as a permanent legacy.

The increase in the quantity of money, which takes place cumulatively as long as the deficit is running, will tend to produce a fall in the rate of interest and (unless confidence has been badly shaken) the effects of an increase in investment, induced by lower interest rates, will be superimposed upon the direct effects of the budget deficit in increasing consumption.

At first there will be a drag upon the fall in the rate of interest because the direct effect of the budget deficit in increasing incomes raises the demand for money, since the requirements of the active circulation depend upon the level of income. But the increase in demand for money will be very slight (so long as money wages do not rise) compared to the increase in supply, and it is a once-and-for-all effect, while the increase in the supply of money is cumulative.

Suppose, for instance, that the Multiplier is 3, and that the active circulation increases by £1 million for every £4 million a year of income. Then a budget deficit at the rate of, say, £12 million a year will lead to an increase in income of £36 million a year (because the Multiplier is 3) and consequently to an increase in the active circulation of £9 million. But the loans of the Central Bank to the government are increasing "cash" at the rate of £1 million a month, so that, if the banks maintain a ratio of cash to other assets of 1 to 9, one month's deficit will lead to an increase of deposits of £10 million, and already before a month has elapsed enough new money will have been created to meet the increase of £9 million in the active circulation. In the early part of the month there is a tendency for the rate of interest to rise, but this tendency is quickly overcome and reversed as the increase in the quantity of money accumulates.

The whole difference between a budget deficit financed by creating money and one financed by ordinary borrowing lies in this reaction upon the rate of interest.

In our numerical example we have taken money wages as constant. A rise in wages enhances the increase in the demand for money due to increased activity, and if unemployment falls so low, under the influence of the deficit, that a rapid rise in money wages sets in, the demand for money may increase to any extent, and may rush ahead of the increase in supply, so that the rate of interest is pushed sharply upward. This situation—a budget deficit financed by borrowing from the Central Bank, unemployment tending to disappear, money wages rising rapidly, an increasing supply of money lagging behind the increase in incomes, and a violent rise in the rate of interest—was characteristic of the later phase of the great German inflation of 1921-3.

Precisely the same consequences follow if the government meets its deficit simply by printing legal-tender notes as if it meets it by borrowing from the Central Bank. For the public is not obliged to hold more notes merely because more have been printed. Notes which the public do not require are deposited in the banks; the cash of the banks is consequently increased just as it is by an increase in Central Bank assets, and a tendency for the rate of interest to fall is super-imposed upon the direct effect of a deficit in increasing activity.

A Social Dividend

In the light of the foregoing analysis we can discuss the proposal to institute a Social Dividend financed by creating money. Under this scheme every citizen would receive a note for, say, £1 by the first post every Saturday, the new notes being printed as required. To conventional minds this scheme sounds altogether too fantastic to be taken seriously, and its advocates have done it some dis-service by the exceedingly complicated and unconvincing arguments which they use in support of it. But all the same it recommends itself to common sense. If there is unemployment on the one hand and unsatisfied needs on the other, why should not the two be brought together, by the simple device of providing the needy with purchasing power to consume the products of the unemployed?

How would such a scheme work out ? In practice (as some tentative experiments in this direction have already shown) it is likely to run upon the rocks through raising opposition from powerful financial interests, but, assuming that it is allowed to work smoothly, it would produce the desired effect of increasing consumption, and therefore employment, in just the same way as an ordinary budget deficit does. The extra pound-a-weeks would be spent, all or in part, upon food and clothes and amusements, trade would prosper, prices rise and unemployment fall. Further, the cumulative increase in the stock of money would bring about a fall in the rate of interest (provided panic was avoided) and so encourage investment, thus giving a further stimulus to activity.

The drawback of the scheme lies in the fact that it robs the monetary authorities of all their power, for while it is in force they can no longer control the quantity of money. When unemployment has been reduced to a minimum and no further increase in real income is possible, a rapid rise in money wages is likely to set in. But still week by week the cumulative increase in the quantity of money would continue, and there would be no defence against the violent rise in prices, collapse of the exchange and general confusion associated with galloping inflation.

Economic life presents us always with a choice of evils, and differences between the orthodox bankers and the currency reformers arise because each chooses a different evil. The bankers are afraid, above everything, of inflation, and are light-hearted in allowing unemployment to occur; currency enthusiasts, on the other hand, see the evils of unemployment and mock at the dangers of inflation; while both differ from more radical reformers in hoping to preserve or to patch up the system of private enterprise, rather than to recast it altogether.

APPENDIX

The Quantity Theory of Money

Discussions of prices and trade activity are often conducted in terms of what is known as the " Quantity Theory of Money ". This is a somewhat misleading title, for actually there is nothing in it that can strictly be called a theory. There is, firstly, the view that an increase in the quantity of money is likely to lead to a rise in prices. We have seen why this view is in general correct—an increase in the quantity of money tends to reduce the rate of interest, a fall in the rate of interest promotes investment, an increase in investment leads to a general increase in activity, and an increase in activity is accompanied by a rise in prices—but a vague general statement that an increase in the quantity of money is likely to lead to a rise in prices cannot properly be described as a theory of money. Secondly, there is a method of approaching the

93

problems of prices by means of an equation involving the quantity of money. This is not a theory of money, but a particular method of analysis.

The simplest form of the Quantity Equation is $MV = PT$. M is the quantity of money (coins, notes and bank deposits), P is an index of the general level of prices, and T is an index of the volume of transactions per unit of time. V is the velocity of circulation; it represents the number of times that a unit of money, on average, is used to make a transaction in the unit of time. If T represents transactions per year, V is the number of times that a unit of money changes hands during a year. If T is reckoned for a week, V is the number of times that a unit of money changes hands in a week; and so forth. If we reckon by the year, PT (the annual value of transactions) is, say, £50,000 million. Then if M, the quantity of money, is, say, £2000 million, V is equal to 25. If we reckon by the week V is equal to roughly $\frac{1}{2}$, and so forth.

Now it is clearly true that $MV = PT$, for PT is the value of the sum of all transactions made during the period with the aid of money, and MV is the sum of all the units of money used in making those transactions. The two are equal because they are two sides of the same thing. But for that very reason the equation cannot possibly tell us anything that we do not know already. We can see from the equation that if, for instance, something happens to raise T, then either P must fall, or M or V must rise. In fact we know (though the equation itself cannot tell us) that in reality a rise in T, the volume of transactions, is normally accompanied by a rise, not a fall, in prices. We can then proceed with this knowledge to say that if something happens to increase T, PT will increase by more. Now the equation tells us that if PT increases either M or V must increase. PT is determined, roughly speaking, by the level of trade activity, and M is controlled by the banking system. We can therefore proceed to say that if something happens to increase PT, but the banks do not increase M, then V must rise.

The argument of Chapter VIII enables us to see how this comes about. If something happens to increase trade activity the demand for money in the active circulation is increased. If the banks do not increase the total amount of money, the rate of interest rises, and, it being now less worth while to hold wealth in the form of money instead of in securities, inactive deposits are reduced as much as the active deposits have increased. The average velocity of circulation of money is therefore raised. Thus an increase in V is brought about as a consequence of an increase in PT. This is all very well, but we have been telling the equation what is happening, it has not been telling us.

More often the equation is read right-handed, thus : if M is increased, then unless V falls in the same proportion, PT must rise. This sounds more helpful, but in fact it obscures the real point. For, as we have seen, an increase in the quantity of money produces its effect upon trade activity by way of a reduction in the rate of interest. Thus it shows itself in the first instance, before PT has had time to alter, precisely in a fall in V. When the quantity of money is increased by the banks buying securities, the whole increase goes immediately into the inactive deposits, where its velocity is zero, and the average velocity of circulation is reduced in exact proportion to the increase in the quantity of money. It is only after the fall in the rate of interest which accompanies an increase in the inactive circulation has had time to produce its effect upon trade activity, and so upon PT, that the increase in M leads to an increase in MV.

No one who understands the rules of logic ever expected a truism, such as $MV = PT$, to tell us anything that we do not know without it, but in inexpert hands the Quantity Equation can lead to great confusion. There are two main criticisms on the habits of thought which it fosters. First, it leads people to discuss changes of prices without making the vital distinction between a change due to a change on the side of demand, such as the rise in prices which accompanies an increase in investment or a reduction in thriftiness, and a change of prices due to a change on the side of supply, such as the rise in prices which is produced by a rise in money wages. Second, it leads people to attribute some kind of direct influence upon prices to changes in the quantity of money, so that some writers seem to suggest that bank-notes have feet, and run into the shops and bid up prices as soon as they are printed. Changes in the quantity of money are of the utmost importance, but their importance lies in their influence upon the rate of interest, and a theory of money which does not mention the rate of interest is not a theory of money at all.

For detailed discussion of changes in trade activity the Quantity Equation is a weak and treacherous instrument. But when we are concerned with broad problems of the movement of prices over the course of generations, it comes into its own. For, as we have seen, an increase in the quantity of money, by lowering the rate of interest and promoting trade activity, leads to a rise in money wages, and since it is easier to raise wages than to lower them, each burst of activity leaves behind a permanent legacy of raised prices. On the other hand if the quantity of money refuses to increase, when population and the general volume of activity is increasing, then the rate of interest will be kept at a high level, trade will be chronically stagnant, workers will be in a weak position *vis-à-vis* employers, and money wages will be stationary or will even tend to fall. Thus the quantity of money exercises a preponderating influence upon the broad movements of prices over the course of history.

CHAPTER XI

FOREIGN TRADE

Foreign Investment

NATIONAL boundaries have for the most part been ignored in the foregoing argument. We must now examine certain questions from the point of view of a single country. First of all we must consider the balance of trade, that is to say the surplus of exports over imports (or of imports over exports). The items composing the balance of trade include both " visible " imports and exports, that is, physical goods moved across national boundaries, and " invisible " imports and exports, such as shipping services, interest on loans, and tourist expenditure, involving payments from the nationals of one country to the nationals of another. It represents the balance of payments on income account between one country and the rest of the world, as opposed to the capital account, represented by international lending and borrowing.

Now, from the point of view of one country, an excess of exports over imports has all the characteristics of investment. Incomes earned by selling goods to foreigners, just like incomes earned by making capital goods, add to the demand for home-produced consumption goods without adding to the supply currently available to be consumed, while home-earned income expended upon foreign-produced goods is subtracted from the demand for home-produced goods. Thus an increase in exports or a decrease in imports sets the Multiplier to work, creates secondary employment and brings about an increase in home income and home saving; in short, produces all the effects upon home activity of an increase in investment.

At the same time, when exports exceed imports the citizens of the rest of the world are, on balance, becoming indebted to the citizens of the home country, for they are consuming more home-produced goods than they are paying for currently. Citizens of the home country are therefore acquiring foreign securities at a rate equal to the excess of exports over imports. Thus the surplus of exports, which represents the *foreign investment* of the home country, adds to the wealth of the home community, and in this respect also it resembles the creation of capital goods.

But from the point of view of the world as a whole the foreign investment of one country is not investment at all. If one country increases its surplus of exports to the rest of the world, the rest of the world must increase its surplus of imports from that country to an equal extent, and there is an increase of unemployment in the rest of the world which offsets the increase of

235329

employment in that country. Moreover, as citizens of that country increase their holding of securities representing loans to the rest of the world, the citizens of the rest of the world are increasing their indebtedness to that country, and for the world as a whole there is no increase in wealth.

HOME ACTIVITY AND FOREIGN INVESTMENT

An increase in activity inside one country generally leads to a decline in its foreign investment. For when larger incomes are being earned there is an increase in expenditure, of which part falls upon foreign goods. When house-building increases at home the newly employed labourer buys more American tinned fruit, the foreman can afford petrol for his motor-bicycle and the contractor takes his holiday on the Riviera. The demand for imports is increased, while nothing has happened to cause a corresponding expansion of exports, so that foreign investment falls off as home investment increases. This is merely another way of putting the fact, which we observed earlier, that the Multiplier for one country is less than for the world as a whole.

If the reduction of unemployment at home leads to a rise in money wages then foreign investment is still further reduced. Money incomes at home are raised, while the prices of foreign goods are unchanged, so that more of them will be purchased. Further, the rise in home wages raises the price of home-produced goods and gives a competitive advantage to foreign goods. At the same time, costs of export goods are raised so that less can be sold. In short, a rise in money wages in one country causes an increase in imports for that country and a decline in exports, so that its rate of foreign investment falls off.

If any one country goes far ahead of the rest in increasing home investment it loses a large part of the benefit, both of increased employment and of increased wealth, through the decline in foreign investment which an increase in home investment brings about.

The importance of this consideration obviously depends upon the extent to which a particular country is engaged in foreign trade. A small, highly specialised country, which imports a large part of what it consumes and exports a large part of what it produces, suffers a severe loss of foreign investment when home investment increases, while a large, almost self-supporting country is little affected.

PUBLIC WORKS IN ONE COUNTRY

We must now modify the statement that public works in slump conditions involve no real cost at all to the community which makes them. This is true for a closed community, but for a single country trading with the rest of the world the loss of foreign investment must be taken into account. Thus, instead of saying that the real cost of public works to the community is nil, because the resources employed would have stood idle if the public works had not been undertaken, we must say that the real cost lies in the foreign investment which would have taken place if the public works had not been made, and does not take place when they are made. It is therefore not the case that public works are worth undertaking from a purely national point of view even if they are of no more use than the Tower of Babel. But so long as they have even a moderate value the case for undertaking them remains strong. Suppose that public works, involving an outlay of £100 million, cause a loss of foreign investment, by reducing exports and increasing imports, of £25 million. Then if the real value of the works to the community is reckoned to be not less than £25 million they are still worth undertaking for their own sake, quite apart from the benefits of increased employment which are enjoyed while they are being carried out.

THE FOREIGN EXCHANGES

The rate of exchange between currencies is determined by the supply and demand for home currency in terms of foreign currencies. Foreign currency is required by home citizens in order to pay their debts abroad, that is to pay for imports, or to make loans abroad, while home currency is required by foreigners to pay for exports from the home country or to make loans to the home country. An increase in the surplus of exports over imports leads to an increase in the foreign demand for home currency relatively to the supply, and so tends to raise the exchange rate, while an increase in the desire of home citizens to lend abroad (to purchase foreign securities) increases the demand for foreign currency and tends to lower the exchange rate. The exchange is in equilibrium, tending neither to rise nor to fall, when, at the ruling rate, the surplus of exports over imports is equal to the net amount of foreign lending, or the surplus of imports is equal to the net amount of foreign borrowing, as the case may be.

We have seen that an increase in activity in one country leads to a decline in the surplus of exports. It therefore tends to weaken the exchange rate. If the exchange rate is allowed to fall, home industries are protected and export industries stimulated, for, with a lower exchange rate and the same internal prices at home and abroad, foreign goods are dearer at home and home goods cheaper abroad. The fall in exchange therefore acts as a break upon the decline in foreign investment which takes place when home investment increases, and keeps a larger share of secondary employment within the home country. It might be argued therefore that a fall in the exchange rate is an excellent thing. But there are some circumstances in which it cannot be allowed to occur.

First of all, if the country is committed to the gold standard the monetary authorities are obliged to keep the exchange steady. To adhere to the gold standard means that the monetary authorities offer to buy and sell gold at a fixed price in terms of the home currency. Now, when the exchange rate falls below the parity set by the fixed gold value of the home currency relatively to the gold value of foreign currencies, it becomes profitable to buy gold at the fixed home price and sell it at the fixed foreign price, using the foreign currency so obtained to buy home currency at the depreciated rate, thus making a profit on the round trip. This very fact prevents the exchange rate from falling below the gold parity by more than the narrow margin which is sufficient to cover the expenses of such operations, but at the same time it means that when the exchange rate tends to be weak the monetary authorities are in danger of losing all their gold. And it is necessary for them to maintain a reserve of gold in order to meet their obligation to sell gold to all comers. Therefore it is necessary for them to create conditions in which the exchange rate does not tend to fall.

Even if the strict obligations of the gold standard are not in force the authorities may be reluctant to allow the exchange to fall, from fear of provoking foreign countries to retaliate. Moreover there is always a danger that too sharp a fall in the exchange rate may lead to complete collapse. For if the initial fall in the exchange rate is taken by speculators as a sign that a further fall is coming, they begin to buy foreign currency, hoping for a profit when it appreciates, and so precipitate a violent fall in the exchange value of the home currency. A mild dose of exchange depreciation, in suitable conditions, may be beneficial to the home country, but a sudden and drastic fall is highly undesirable, and the authorities regard it as their duty to avoid it at all costs. For these reasons, amongst others, the monetary authorities may feel obliged to prevent a fall in the exchange rate from taking place.

The weapon by which the authorities control the foreign exchange is the rate of interest. A rise in the home rate of interest has a triple effect upon the exchanges. First, it inclines foreigners to lend to the home country, and disinclines home citizens to lend abroad. It therefore increases the demand for home currency relatively to the supply, and strengthens the exchange. This reaction is immediate. As times goes by a second influence comes into operation. With a higher rate of interest investment at home falls off, and employment and incomes decline. This, as we have seen, curtails expenditure upon imports along with expenditure on home goods, and so increases the surplus of exports. The exchange is thus strengthened. Finally, but only after the elapse of many wretched years, money wages at home may be driven down by the pressure of unemployment. Export industries are then stimulated and it is possible to permit a higher level of home consumption without imperilling the exchange. The rate of interest, therefore, can be lowered again when a sufficient fall in money wages has taken place. Thus an increase of prosperity at home weakens the exchange rate and the exchange rate can be restored only by killing prosperity.

EXPANSION IN ONE COUNTRY

We can now see how the authorities of any one country are limited in their power to foster a high level of employment at home. Anything which they do to stimulate activity at home leads to trouble with the exchange rate. Public works, redistributional taxation, a budget deficit, all lead, by increasing home consumption, to an increase in imports relatively to exports, a decline in the balance of trade, and consequently a fall in the exchange rate. Thus the national authorities must be cautious in considering how far it is safe to go, and even when they feel a sincere desire to reduce unemployment at home they may have a very limited power to do so.

But the dangers of an expansionist policy are sometimes exaggerated, as an excuse for inaction. The country which brings about an increase in activity at home is benefiting the rest of the world, for the very fact that its demand for import goods rises with increased home employment means that activity in other countries is increased. This improvement may lead to a revival of optimism and set home investment on foot in those countries also. The home country will then benefit in its turn from increased activity in the rest of the world. Thus any one important country which takes a bold course may lead the world to prosperity, while if each sits timidly waiting for some other to begin, all must continue in misery.

THE RATE OF INTEREST IN ONE COUNTRY

Each national government is limited in its power to carry out expansionist policies such as public works schemes. A national monetary authority is even more circumscribed in its power to control the home rate of interest. If the rate of interest is lowered in one country the exchange is weakened for two reasons. Not only does the consequent increase in home investment lead to a decline in the balance of trade, but also the relative reduction in home interest rates encourages foreign lending, for a better return can now be obtained abroad than at home. Thus any one national authority which endeavours to foster home activity by reducing the rate of interest is in danger of precipitating a collapse of the exchange rate, and no one is able to go far unless the rest are prepared to follow.

Each one claims excuse for maintaining the rate of interest at a level which causes unemployment in the fact that none is free to act alone.

But a cautious spirit in each individually is damaging to all collectively. A high rate of interest in any one country weakens the exchanges of the rest (and attracts gold from them if the gold standard is in force). They are driven to defend their exchange rates (and protect their gold reserves) by raising their own interest rates, and so, the world over, the rate of interest is driven up, investment is discouraged, unemployment increases, and misery spreads from one country to another. A share in the sufferings imposed upon the world by a policy of high interest rates comes home to roost to the country which starts the movement, and too narrow a regard for the national advantage may defeat its own ends. Conversely, any one country which lowers its interest rate is benefiting the world, and the advantages of a bold policy come home to roost as well as the evils of timidity.

Economic Nationalism

Unfortunately the governments of the world at the present time appear more prone to snatch an advantage for their own country at the expense of the rest of the world than to carry out policies which benefit the world as a whole. When a severe slump sets in there is unemployment and loss of income in each country. In each country a clamour is raised to defend home industry against foreign competition, and a variety of schemes are devised to reduce imports and increase exports so as to mitigate the decline in home activity.

Of these schemes a tariff upon imports is the most common. The object of a protective tariff is to deflect demand from foreign to home goods and so to increase profits and employment in home industries. An increase in employment in the protected industries leads in the usual way to secondary employment in home consumption-good industries, and to some extent counteracts the effects of the slump.

A competitive advantage can also be obtained for one country by devaluing its exchange, for, as we have seen, this fosters exports, by making home goods cheaper to foreigners, and protects home industry, by making foreign goods dearer at home. Similarly an advantage can be gained by cutting wages in the home country. An all-round reduction in wages in one country relatively to the rest of the world increases its exports, by making them cheaper, and curtails its imports, by reducing home incomes and prices of home-produced goods relatively to the prices of goods from the outside world. Thus a fall in the exchange rate (provided it does not go too far), or a reduction in wages, improves the balance of trade and increases employment in the country which carries it out.

For every increase of employment at home there is a corresponding increase of unemployment abroad, where export industries have lost their markets and home industries are exposed to competition from cheap imports. For the rest of the world slump conditions become still more severe. From a purely nationalist point of view this in itself is of no importance—if the un employed are foreigners they are no concern of ours—but it leads to consequences of which the most hard-bitten nationalist must take account. For other countries, finding themselves in a more wretched plight than ever, will have still stronger motives for protecting themselves, by tariffs, devaluation or wage cuts. Retaliation will begin, and before long all the nations of the world will be playing a frantic game of beggar-my-neighbour. As soon as one snatches an advantage it is grabbed back by another, and each is powerless to stand out when the others have begun, for any one nation which refused to join in the game would rapidly be beggared by its less scrupulous neighbours.

Considered collectively all are worse off than before they began. International trade is choked in an entanglement of tariffs, quotas and embargoes and all the benefits of international division of labour are lost to the world. The advantages of exchange stability are forgone. And competition in forcing down wages leads to the waste and bitterness of strikes, the social injustice of arbitrary changes in relative wage rates, and the enhanced burden of indebtedness which follows from a general fall in all values save those fixed in terms of money. All this leaves an evil legacy behind, and even when a world revival sets in and the nations cease their scramble for international trade, the ill effects of the beggar-my-neighbour policies remain and cannot quickly be undone.

APPENDIX

The Free Trade Controversy

There is a perennial controversy over the merits of free trade and protection, which has never been resolved because, as so often happens, the contestants are talking at cross purposes. The strong point of the free trade case is that artificial barriers to trade lead to inefficiency of production. There is a presumption that the free play of competition will sort out industries as between the various regions of the world in a more economic manner than the whims of politicians. The very fact that an industry needs to be protected in one country shows that it can be conducted more efficiently elsewhere, and protective policies sacrifice the advantage of division of labour between nations, cause economic resources to be used less productively than they might, and so impoverish the world.

The strong point of the protectionist argument is that when home industry is suffering from foreign competition a duty on imports will lead to an increase in the demand for home products, and so increase activity, employment and profits at home.

Now, there is nothing incompatible in these two arguments. The free trade argument shows that tariffs reduce output per man, and the protectionist argument shows that they increase the number of men employed (in the home country—unemployment abroad does not weigh with protectionists). The relative importance of the two arguments varies with the prevalence of unemployment, and, as we have seen, it is in times of depression that the nations of the world are most inclined to resort to protectionist policies. There must always be differences of opinion as to what is the most desirable policy at any moment, but there is no need for dispute about the principles involved.

Unfortunately some fanatical free-traders, over-anxious to establish what they hold to be a righteous cause, have refused to allow any validity at all to the protectionist case, and go so far as actually to deny that a tariff can increase employment in the country that imposes it. Their argument runs as follows: Exports pay for imports, and if imports are cut down, exports must fall off equally. Thus they appear to deny that foreign investment can take place at all— that there can ever be a surplus of exports. When it is pointed out that a surplus of exports can in fact occur, and that the effect of a tariff is to increase it, they fall back upon a further argument. A surplus of exports entails a corresponding amount of lending from the home country to the rest of the world. An increase in the surplus of exports, by increasing foreign lending, depletes the funds available for home industry, and causes home investment to fall off as much as foreign investment increases.

Thus they overlook the fact that an increase in investment leads to an increase in activity and incomes, and consequently to an increase in saving. The increase in foreign investment itself calls into existence the additional savings required to finance it, and there is no reason why home investment should fall off. Quite the contrary. The decline in imports due to the tariff strengthens the exchange rate and so creates a situation favourable to a fall in the rate of interest, while the increased prosperity of home industry raises prospective profits on capital at home, so that an increase, rather than a decline, in home investment is likely to set in.

If a very high level of employment obtains in the home country the simple argument that " exports pay for imports " comes into its own, for in that case there are no idle resources to be called into employment in the protected home industries, and home industries can expand, to replace imports, only in so far as export industries contract and release labour for their use. But when unemployment is negligible the protectionist argument is irrelevant. Thus the free-traders' argument is valid only when no argument is needed at all.

It is unfortunate for the cause of free trade that such arguments should have been used in its defence, for the true objection to protectionism— that it fosters the interests of each country at the expense of the rest, and so sets the world by the ears—is only obscured by denying that even one country can obtain an advantage from it.

CHAPTER XII

CHANGES IN EMPLOYMENT

THE TRADE CYCLE

WE have now collected the pieces of our jig-saw puzzle, and we must fit them together to form a picture of the fluctuations in employment to which a system of private enterprise is subject.

At any moment trade is always either improving or relapsing, and in the real world "normal times" never come; we must therefore make an arbitrary choice as to where to take up our story. The most convenient place to begin is the early stage of a trade revival. The rate of investment begins to rise, and consequently activity in the consumption-good industries increases, to the extent dictated by the size of the Multiplier. As output is increasing investment in working capital takes place, and gives a further fillip to activity. Now the general state of trade has improved and profits are increasing. The lethargy and despair of the slump period leave the souls of entrepreneurs, and their views of future profits begin to be coloured by the higher level of profits ruling in the present. A further expansion of investment therefore takes place. New equipment is ordered to provide for the

higher rate of output and new concerns spring
up to take advantage of expanding demand. With
the higher level of investment, and consequently
of expenditure, profits are again increased, prospects are further improved, new schemes of
investment undertaken, and the upward movement feeds on itself.

This process may continue over the course of
several years. But all the time the products of
investment are accumulating—buildings, equipment, ships, improvements to land, and durable
capital goods of all kinds are coming into use,
and the competition of each new arrival reduces
the level of profits for those already in existence.
The expansion of investment slows down.

Now, the tragedy of investment is that (unless
stimulants are applied) it can never remain at a
constant level. For if the rate of investment one
year is the same as the last, then, generally
speaking, the level of employment and incomes
and therefore the level of demand for goods will
be the same in the second year as in the first. But
all the time capital is accumulating, and in the
second year there is a larger amount of equipment available to meet the same demand for
commodities. The rate of profit consequently falls
off, future prospects are dimmed by the decline
in present receipts, and in the third year new
investment appears less attractive to entrepreneurs than in the second.

Once investment begins to decline, the Multiplier is set to work in the downward direction,

consumption falls off, unemployment increases, and activity and profits decline. The prospects of future profits degenerate under the influence of their present decline, investment falls still further, and the downward movement feeds on itself.

But just as the tragedy of investment lies in the fact that it makes durable additions to real wealth, so a paradoxical comfort is to be found in the fact that capital goods are not permanently durable. Obsolescence and wear and tear deplete the stock of capital, and when activity has ruled at its lowest level for a year or two the gradual decline in the supply of efficient equipment raises the level of profit for that which remains. Here and there investment in making good deficiencies begins to take place, and with an increase in the rate of investment the whole story begins again.

This is the rhythm of investment, which is the main force governing the cycle of trade activity. Other movements are superimposed upon the underlying rhythm. As we have seen, there is a tendency for thriftiness in the capitalist class to decline as prosperity increases, under the influence of a Stock Exchange boom, so that the upswing of activity is enhanced by an increase in the ratio of consumption to investment just when investment itself is increasing. The reaction of spirits which sets in when prosperity begins to decline, and Stock Exchange prices fall, enhances the downward movement, and so the oscillations of trade are exaggerated in each direction.

Changes in sentiment further exaggerate the violence of trade oscillations. We have so far described the process of improving and declining trade as though it took place gradually and smoothly, and this would be the case if entrepreneurs at each moment judged the future level of profits mainly by the current level of profits. But if they develop a state of mind in which increasing profits lead them to expect a further increase in the future, and declining profits a further decline, then the oscillations of investment will be exaggerated, and the turning point will come with greater violence. As soon as investment ceases to increase, exaggerated pessimism will take the place of exaggerated optimism and the slump period will be inaugurated by a sudden violent decline in activity instead of a gradual relapse.

The rhythm of thriftiness and the rhythm of expectations exaggerate the effects of the rhythm of investment. Movements of the rate of interest on the other hand come in as a counterweight to the rest. As the level of activity declines the demand for money shrinks, and the rate of interest tends to fall. The decline in investment is therefore less severe than it would be if the rate of interest were constant, and when the bottom is reached recovery sets in sooner. Conversely increasing activity, particularly if it is accompanied by rising money wages, drives up the rate of interest by increasing the demand for money. Consequently the increase in the rate of investment is checked and the period of prosperity curtailed. Thus the rhythm of the rate of interest runs counter to the rhythm of investment and damps down the oscillations of trade.

A movement, in either direction, in one country tends to spread over the world. Booms and slumps are catching, for when activity increases in one country the benefit is felt in others, by way of increased demand for exports, and when activity falls off in one country the rest are impoverished. For any one country the initial upward movement may take the form of increased foreign investment due to a revival of activity abroad.

A movement in the exchange rate may counteract influences coming from the outside world and the infection spreads most easily when the exchanges are stable. When the gold standard system was in full operation the nations of the western economic world moved closely in step with each other, but in the post-war period we have several times seen particular countries insulated from a world slump by a reduced exchange rate, or cut off from the benefits of a world revival by pertinacious adherence to a high rate.

CONTROLLING THE TRADE CYCLE

These movements comprise what is often called the " natural " rhythm of business activity, as opposed to the influences of government or

118

monetary policy. The dichotomy is somewhat artificial, for the actions of governments and monetary authorities are as much a part of nature as the actions of private entrepreneurs ; but the world is growing more conscious of the trade cycle, it is beginning to be regarded as a duty for the authorities to mitigate the violence of booms and slumps by whatever means they may possess, and their actions therefore tend to run counter to the action of private entrepreneurs.

The motive of the authorities for attempting to improve trade during a slump is obvious enough. There are two distinct types of motive for wishing to check a boom. First, it is often argued that boom conditions should be prevented from developing because it is the boom which is the cause of the slump that follows it. In a certain sense this is true, for as we have seen it is the very fact that a high rate of capital accumulation takes place in the boom which prevents the boom from continuing. But it does not follow that booms ought to be eliminated. There are not two kinds of investment—good investment which does not bring on a decline in activity and bad investment which does. All investment is good in that it promotes activity while it is going on and adds to wealth when it is completed. All is bad in the sense that it cannot last and must be followed by a decline in activity. It is impossible to get rid of the bad features of investment without sacrificing the good features, and to stabilise trade by means of

110

eliminating booms would merely be to enforce a permanent slump. It may, indeed, be argued that the average of prosperity, one year with another, would be higher if a moderate level of prosperity were exchanged for a high level at some times and a low level at others, though, even if this could be established, a policy of maintaining unemployment permanently at a little below its present average level is not one that can be recommended with much enthusiasm. But whatever may be the merits of the argument, the notion that a boom is to be feared as a cause of depression has considerable influence in inclining the authorities to check the development of boom conditions when they begin to appear.

The second motive for wishing to damp down boom conditions is the fear of inflation. Inflation has become a stock bogy to such an extent that even in the depths of depression in 1931 it was not thought ridiculous to frighten the public by parading it, but actually no case of extreme inflation has been known to occur in normal circumstances. Inflation as we have seen requires two conditions : first, that the level of unemployment has fallen so low that a violent and irresistible rise in money wages takes place ; and second, that something has occurred to remove the stopper normally provided by a limited quantity of money, which ensures that the rate of interest shall be pushed up, and investment consequently checked, when the rise in money wages begins. Wars and revolutions have frequently led to violent inflation, but in times of peace with a stable government and a competent monetary authority it is little to be feared. All the same the dread of inflation has such a strong hold upon the minds of the authorities that it plays an important part in inclining them to use their influence to prevent trade conditions from becoming what they regard as dangerously good.

note Apart from beggar-my-neighbour policies, the two chief weapons of the authorities for counteracting booms and slumps are the rate of interest and public investment. The monetary authorities normally try to foster the remedial action of the rate of interest by deliberately increasing the quantity of money when activity has fallen to a low level, and restricting it when the boom is at its height, thus enhancing the " natural " movements in the rate of interest. It is found that such action as the authorities normally take is not sufficient to induce a steady rate of investment, for once pessimism has taken hold of the entrepreneurs a moderate fall in the rate of interest is not sufficient to restore the inducement to invest, and when they are dazzled by golden visions of profit a moderate rise in the rate of interest will not check their enthusiasm. But the movements of the rate of interest induced by the authorities at least tell in the direction of damping down oscillations of trade.

Public works policy has long been advocated as a corrective to the trade cycle. The ideal policy which has been put forward is for plans to be worked out many years in advance of requirements, and for the rate at which they are carried out to be adjusted so as to counteract the movements of private investment. This policy has now won almost universal acceptance in principle but it has yet to be seen in full action. A considerable share in the revival of trade which began in 1933 is to be attributed to the deliberate efforts of a number of governments to foster investment. But in the early part of 1937, when talk of a boom began to be common and a reduction in public investment was advocated, the governments of the world were concentrating their energies on an armaments race, so that public investment increased still further just at the time when a revival in private investment was well under way.

Long-Period Influences

The regular pattern of the trade cycle is interrupted by particular events—a war, a good harvest, a political crisis, an important invention or the discovery of a new gold-field—which jerk the movement of trade from its normal course, so that the path which it follows is full of irregularities. The history of trade presents the spectacle of a strong tendency to regular oscillations, interrupted by sporadic movements in one direction or another.

Further, the oscillations of the trade cycle overlie deeper influences. Increasing population,

122

a rapid succession of inventions and opportunities for exploiting new territories, give buoyancy to the profitability of capital and provide an ever-renewed stimulus to investment.

When these sources of demand for capital are lacking it appears that the motive for investment must be chronically weak, so that slumps are deep and prolonged, and moderate prosperity is hailed by contrast as a boom. Since the increase in population is rapidly approaching its end in the western world, no fresh continents remain to be discovered, and a new age of invention comparable with the nineteenth century is scarcely to be hoped for, it appears that in the near future powerful stimulants will have to be applied to the economic system if chronic unemployment is to be avoided.

A long-run fall in the rate of interest would do much to stimulate private investment, while an extension of public investment could make up for its deficiencies, and a drastic policy of redistribution of income would increase consumption, and reduce the amount of investment necessary to preserve a reasonable level of employment. All these policies meet with serious difficulties and have to contend with violent opposition, and it remains to be seen whether it is possible for the present economic system to adapt itself to the requirements of the future.

CHAPTER XIII

CONTROVERSY IN ECONOMICS

TYPES OF CONTROVERSY

THE subject-matter of this book has been the battle-ground of controversy since thinking about economic affairs first began, and the controversy is still raging. But in a subject of this sort there can be no ground for controversy. Differences of opinion there may be, but all controversies should be capable of resolution. The rules of logic and the laws of evidence are the same for everyone, and in the nature of the case there can be nothing to dispute about.

Controversies arise for five main reasons. First, they occur when the two parties fail to understand each other. Here patience and toleration should provide a cure. Second, controversies occur in which one (or both) of the parties has made an error of logic. Here the spectators at least should be able to decide on which side reason lies. Third, the two parties may be making, unwittingly, different assumptions, and each maintaining something which is correct on the appropriate assumptions. The two knights are disputing as to whether the shield is black or white, when one side of the shield is black and the other side white. Here the remedy is to discover the assumptions and to set each argument out in a manner which makes clear that it is not inconsistent with the other. Fourth, there may not be sufficient evidence to settle a question of fact conclusively one way or the other. Here the remedy is for each party to preserve an open mind and to assist in the search for further evidence. Fifth, there may be differences of opinion as to what is a desirable state of affairs. Here no resolution is possible, since judgments of ultimate values cannot be settled by any purely intellectual process. But dispute is idle.

It is the fifth source of controversy which keeps all the rest alive. When some important issue of public policy is at stake the disputants each clings desperately to his own opinion. Each refuses to understand the other, for fear that if he understood he might be compelled to make some concession. Each persists in his errors, for he who is convinced against his will is of the same opinion still. Each refuses to reconsider his assumptions for fear of being obliged to admit that his assumptions do not conform to reality. Each reads the incomplete evidence in his own favour.

Controversies in economics persist, not because economists are necessarily less intelligent or more bad-tempered than the rest of mankind, but because the issues involved arouse strong feeling. A bad argument which appears to favour a desired policy is obstinately and passionately upheld in face of a better argument that appears to tell against it. But argument in the nature of the case can make no difference to ultimate judgments based on interest or moral feeling. The ideal is to set out all the arguments fairly on their merits, and agree to differ about ultimate values.

Sources of Controversy

On questions of policy the differences can never be resolved. Even such an apparently simple problem as, for instance, the extension of public works as a remedy for unemployment, is found to give rise to violent conflicts of interest.

It appears at first sight as though, if governments can reduce unemployment, and add to real wealth, by undertaking investment, it must be quite unambiguously beneficial for them to do so. But even on this question acute differences of opinion arise. We have seen that the community as a whole is enriched by public works undertaken during a slump. But many individuals in the community find that they suffer from such a policy. Those who are enriched by additional saving during the period of profits induced by public works are not necessarily, man for man, the same individuals who will have to pay higher taxes in the future to provide interest on the larger public debt. Anyone who shares more (or fears he may share more) in the additional future taxation than in the additional present profit will have a motive for opposing the scheme. Individuals whose incomes are

126

legally fixed in terms of money suffer from a rise
of prices when employment increases. Governments who are opposed in principle to extending
the sphere of socialism prefer that there should
be less real capital in existence rather than that
they should be saddled with the ownership of
more capital. Revolutionaries who regard unemployment as only one of the evils of a system
of private enterprise are not anxious for capitalist governments to learn the trick of reducing
fluctuations in trade, and so deprive them of the
most obvious, though not the most fundamental,
of their objections to the system. The adherents
of *laisser-faire*, on the other hand, fear that, if it
once became clear to the public that state interference can reduce unemployment, the public
might begin to think that state interference
could do much else besides.

All these conflicts are raised even by the
simple question of public works policy. How
much the more by questions involving reductions in inequality of income.

Academic disputes amongst economists are
apt to appear to the layman as idle and remote
as the dispute as to how many angels can stand
on a pin. But the academic disputes about x's
and y's are in reality the surface ripples of these
deep-lying conflicts (if they were not so, all the
questions would have been settled long ago).
The controversies and the political issues are
bound up together. Both have been avoided as
far as possible in this book.

Printed in Great Britain by R. & R. CLARK, LIMITED, *Edinburgh*

BY JOAN ROBINSON

THE ECONOMICS
OF IMPERFECT COMPETITION

8vo. **18s.** net.

"Starting from the simple definitions of monopoly equilibrium that Marshall laid down, Mrs. Robinson has written a book that may well begin a new period of economic thought."—*The Economist*.

"This book is a great achievement. . . . It opens a new chapter in economic science."

COLIN CLARK in *The Cambridge Review*.

"Mrs. Robinson's book is an important economic event. . . . Mrs. Robinson has set economic theory on a new road, with a more useful destination. It is just what was wanted."—*The Financial News*.

ESSAYS IN THE
THEORY OF EMPLOYMENT

8vo. **8s. 6d.** net.

"This distinguished collection of essays, like the author's previous publications, displays all the marks of independent and original thought. . . . Some important conclusions of a practical nature are reached. . . . The third section of the book contains two admirable essays on 'The Foreign Exchanges' and on 'Beggar-my-Neighbour Remedies for Unemployment.' The essay on the foreign exchanges is a model of lucidity and comprehensiveness, theoretically elegant and practically wise, while the second essay deals with the very important distinction between different types of policies taken to relieve unemployment."

The Times Literary Supplement.

"These essays should be of great value to those who, having read Mr. Keynes' *General Theory*, wish to pursue further the line of approach which he has worked out."

The Cambridge Review.

MACMILLAN AND CO. LTD., LONDON

NEW WORKS ON ECONOMICS

SOCIALISM VERSUS CAPITALISM. By
A. C. Pigou, M.A., Professor of Political Economy
in the University of Cambridge. 4s. 6d. net.

PERSONS AND PERIODS. By G. D. H. Cole.
12s. 6d. net.

A collection of essays and studies dealing mainly with
social change in England since the beginning of the
eighteenth century.

FOREIGN BALANCES. By Paul Einzig.
8s. 6d. net.

SOVIET TRADE AND DISTRIBUTION. By
Leonard E. Hubbard, author of "Soviet Money
and Finance."

NEW MONEY FOR NEW MEN. By
S. S. Metz.

Mr. Metz believes that the community is no longer dis-
posed to regard recurrent trade depression and permanent
unemployment as an immutable feature of a sacrosanct
financial order, and that it is futile to assume they will
acquiesce, in the long run, in piecemeal tinkering.

MATHEMATICAL ANALYSIS FOR ECONO-
MISTS. By R. G. D. Allen. 31s. 6d. net.

COMMERCIAL BANKING LEGISLATION
AND CONTROL. By A. M. Allen, M.A., B.Com.,
Assistant Secretary to the Institute of Bankers;
S. R. Cope, B.Sc. (Econ.) ; L. J. H. Dark, B.Com.;
H. J. Witheridge, B.Com. 18s. net.

MACMILLAN AND CO. LTD., LONDON